Power
Through
Prayer

Power Through Prayer

By Ronald W. Goetsch

Guidelines for

Developing an Effective Prayer Life

Concordia Publishing House · Saint Louis

The Library of Congress has catalogued this book as follows:

Goetsch, Ronald W
    Power through prayer; guidelines for developing an effective prayer life.   Saint Louis, Concordia Pub. House ₁1959₁

    145 p.   19 cm.

1. Prayer.   I. Title.

BV215.G6   264.1   59–7789 ‡

Library of Congress

Table of Contents

Introduction

A shrieking, bloodthirsty mob is hurrying out of Jerusalem pushing before it a man whose crime is that he is a professed disciple and worshiper of the Nazarene, who a few years before had passed through another Jerusalem gate, bearing a cross. The mob is clamoring for the man's death; and the man, already roughed up and bruised, is thrown to the ground. The people draw back a few steps and begin to hurl stones at him. The man prays, and his prayer is a public homage paid to Him for whose sake he is about to die. "Lord Jesus," he prays, "receive my spirit" (Acts 7:59). As the murderous stones are hurled at him with redoubled violence, he succeeds in raising himself to a kneeling position, crying with a loud voice, "Lord, lay not this sin to their charge!" (Acts 7:60). And with this prayer he dies; or rather, as St. Luke has it, he falls asleep. The dying Stephen prays; and as he prays, he dies. There is nothing incredible about this, for Stephen was a Christian.

Among those who were present at that lynching and who were unmoved by this touching prayer and this terrible mangling of a poor human frame was a young man who was especially conspicuous for his eager participation. St. Luke, who chronicled much of his later life, does not say that this young man cast any stones with his own hands. But only too willingly he consented to this death and in a manner even presided at the stoning; for when the accusers, according to custom, prepared to throw the first stones, it was at the feet of this young man that they laid their garments. The young man left the spot "breathing out threatenings and slaughter against the disciples of the Lord" (Acts 9:1). The sight of Christian blood seemed to have given him a thirst for more — and the Christians began to fear Saul.

True to the pattern he had set for himself and eager to ferret out the Christians, Saul went to the high priest at Jerusalem for warrants of arrest of any disciples he might find in his new sphere of activity. Armed with these warrants, he set out for distant Damascus, accompanied by a bodyguard. Not far from Damascus the arrester became the arrested. A flash! A fall! A voice! "Saul, Saul, why persecutest thou Me?" (Acts 9:4). It was a reasonable question — and searching. Astonished and bewildered, Saul asked, "Who art Thou, Lord?" And the Lord answered, "I am Jesus, whom thou persecutest; it is

2

hard for thee to kick against the pricks" (Acts 9:5). Greatly surprised to find that the crucified Jesus was alive, that He completely identified Himself with those who were being persecuted as His disciples, and that he, Saul, was resisting the divine will, Saul, following the first impulse of surrender, cried, "Lord, what wilt Thou have me to do?" And the Lord said unto him, "Arise, and go into the city, and it shall be told thee what thou must do." (Acts 9:6)

Blind, but with the hand of God upon him to guide him, Saul was led to the house of Judas in the street called Straight. There by the goodness of God, who understands the human soul, he was left sightless for three days — alone with his thoughts — and prayers — this young man who till now had been the rising hope of the Pharisees. He had come face to face with the exalted Jesus, and the experience had stricken him to his very soul. And he prayed as he had never prayed before — as he had never been taught to pray. I wonder what Judas of Damascus thought of this strange unbidden guest who spent these three days in his house in fasting and prayer. Did he sometimes tiptoe to the door of Saul's room and listen in amazement to the voice within, now sobbing out a despairing confession, now crying out a supplicating prayer? Who would ever have thought it possible?

Not Ananias.

Ananias also was due for a surprise. The Lord appeared to him in a vision and told him, "Arise, and go into the street which is called Straight, and inquire in the house of Judas for one called Saul of Tarsus;

3

for, behold, he prayeth and hath seen in a vision a man named Ananias coming in and putting his hand on him that he might receive his sight" (Acts 9:11, 12). A Christian one would expect to pray, but surely this was a trap; and Ananias was not to be taken in. "I have heard by many of this man," he countered, "how much evil he hath done to Thy saints at Jerusalem; and here he hath authority from the chief priests to bind all that call on Thy name" (Acts 9: 13, 14). But the Lord silenced him with gentle firmness. "Go thy way; for he is a chosen vessel unto Me to bear My name before the Gentiles and kings and the Children of Israel; for I will show him how great things he must suffer for My name's sake" (Acts 9: 15, 16). A chosen vessel! No wonder he was praying!

With God nothing is impossible. Saul, who before had breathed out threatenings and slaughters, was now breathing out prayers; and his prayers marked him a disciple, who together with the other disciples was soon to be called a Christian. Prayer was an integral part of his first experience as a Christian, and the whole tenor of his subsequent life was fashioned by it. Paul prayed anywhere and everywhere: in the synagog, in the city streets, on country roads, by the seashore, in prison, on board ship, amidst the thronging crowd, or in the company of a faithful few. "Behold, he prayeth," according to the testimony of the Lord Himself, was his first credential as a Christian; and proudly did the Lord call attention to it. Not that he had never prayed before, for he was a Hebrew of the Hebrews and of the strictest sect,

4

a Pharisee; but the content and manner of his prayer now definitely marked him a changed man. And the chosen vessel of the Lord continued instant in prayer.

Has the Lord reason to be proud of us in this respect? We claim to be Christians. We are. Do we pray as Christians? Do we live the prayer life? We ought to. The Lord expects us to.

1.

God's Ordinance of Prayer

God wants us to pray; indeed, He has commanded us to pray.

In 1 Chronicles 16:11 we read, "Seek the Lord and His strength; seek His face continually." This is a command. In Psalm 105:4 the identical command is repeated.

In Psalm 50:15 we read, "Call upon Me in the day of trouble." This is a command. We sometimes lose sight of the command in our joy over the attached promise: "I will deliver thee."

In Isaiah 55:6 we read, "Seek ye the Lord while He may be found; call ye upon Him while He is near." This, too, is a command to pray.

The commands multiply. "Wait on the Lord; be of good courage, and He shall strengthen thine heart;

wait, I say, on the Lord" (Psalm 27:14). "Wait on the Lord, and He shall save thee" (Proverbs 20:22). "Turn thou to thy God; keep mercy and judgment, and wait on thy God continually" (Hosea 12:6). "Ask ye of the Lord" (Zechariah 10:1). "Ask and it shall be given you; seek, and ye shall find; knock, and it shall be opened unto you" (Matthew 7:7; Luke 11:9). "And He spake a parable unto them to this end, that men ought always to pray, and not to faint" (Luke 18:1). "Ask, and ye shall receive" (John 16:24). "Watch and pray, that ye enter not into temptation" (Matthew 26:41). "Continuing instant in prayer" (Romans 12:12). "Praying always with all prayer and supplication in the Spirit and watching thereunto with all perseverance and supplication for all saints" (Ephesians 6:18). "In everything by prayer and supplication with thanksgiving let your requests be made known unto God" (Philippians 4:6). "Pray without ceasing" (1 Thessalonians 5:17). "If any of you lack wisdom, let him ask of God. . . . Is any among you afflicted? Let him pray." (James 1:5; 5:13)

There are many more commands, implied and expressed, all of which may be summarized simply in Luther's words: "He Himself has commanded us so to pray."

Luther was, of course, not the first to recognize and to act upon the Lord's command. The psalmist, appreciating the implication of the Lord's command, writes: "When Thou saidst, Seek ye My face, my heart said unto Thee, Thy face, Lord, will I seek" (Psalm 27:8). And ages before that, before ever these many commands had accumulated, in the days of Enos, son

7

of Seth, "began men to call upon the name of the Lord" (Genesis 4:26). This chain of commands reaches from age to age; and we of this latter age have adopted as our own the following affirmations of Luther in the Large Catechism: "The first thing is to know that it is our duty to pray because of God's commandment"; "Prayer is therefore as strictly and earnestly commanded as all other commandments"; and: "On the commandment on which all saints rest their prayer I, too, rest mine." (*Book of Concord*, pp. 197, 198)

Prayer, then, is not only a privilege which is granted us; it is also a duty which is enjoined upon us. Brownlow Maitland puts it nicely in *In Steps to Faith* (p. 92), when he writes: "To pray, not now and then, or on great occasions only, but constantly, habitually, in regard to everything that bears on his hopes and fears, his joys and sorrows, his trials, endeavors, and aspirations, is not merely a privilege permitted to the servant of Christ, but also a duty enjoined upon him by the law under which he lives. Nothing can be more comprehensive than the words, 'In everything . . . let your requests be made known unto God.'" (Philippians 4:6)

GOD'S ORDINANCE OF PRAYER PREDICATES HIS DESIRE FOR COMMUNION WITH MAN

God's ordinance of prayer predicates His desire for communion with man — the desire of the Infinite to fellowship with the finite. It is true that because of the command of God to pray "it is not left to my

8

will to do it or leave it undone, but prayer shall and must be offered at the risk of God's wrath and displeasure" (*Book of Concord*, p. 197); yet a Christian, insofar as he is a child of God, should above all regard God's command to pray as the gracious condescension of a loving God, who would encourage him to draw close in prayer that He might forgive and bless and fellowship with him, for God is eager to fellowship with man.

Toward the end of the sixth day God had created a world that was perfect and was beautiful in its perfection; but God was not yet finished, for there was lacking a creature with whom He might fellowship. He therefore said, "Let Us make man in Our image, after Our likeness" (Genesis 1:26). He desired a creature with whom He might have things in common. "So God created man in His own image; in the image of God created He him" (Genesis 1:27). He placed man in the Garden of Eden, and in His desire for his fellowship accommodated Himself to the ways of man by "walking in the garden in the cool of the day" (Genesis 3:8). How keen the Lord's disappointment when man so soon fell into sin!

But the Lord God persisted. In love He sought to restore man to the place from which he had fallen — first by way of promise, then by way of fulfillment. He sent His Son, the incarnation and the revelation of His love, to re-establish the privilege of fellowship which man by his sin had forfeited. And St. John, who saw that revelation, writes: "That which we have seen and heard declare we unto you that ye also may have fellowship with us; and truly our fel-

9

lowship is with the Father and with His Son Jesus Christ" (1 John 1:3). The fellowship between God and man has been restored, so much so that St. James exhorts and promises us, "Draw nigh to God, and He will draw nigh to you." (James 4:8)

God's Ordinance of Prayer Predicates the Hunger of the Soul of Man for God

God's ordinance of prayer, however, predicates not only His own desire for communion with man whom He created in His own image but also the hunger of the soul of man for God, his need for divine direction, and his instinctive desire to get in touch with the One who is higher than himself. Saint Augustine expressed the thought in these words: "Thou hast made us for Thyself, O Lord, and our heart is restless until it rests in Thee." And Carlyle in a letter to a friend stated it in this way: "Prayer is and remains the native and deepest impulse of the soul of man."

St. Paul knew and appreciated this hunger, or need, for God that is native in the soul of man. On Mars' Hill he spoke to the Grecian philosophers: "Ye men of Athens, I perceive that in all things ye are too superstitious. For as I passed by and beheld your devotions, I found an altar with this inscription: TO THE UNKNOWN GOD. Whom therefore ye ignorantly worship, Him declare I unto you. God that made the world and all things therein, seeing that He is Lord of heaven and earth, dwelleth not in temples made with hands; neither is worshiped with men's hands,

10

as though He needed anything, seeing He giveth to all life and breath and all things and hath made of one blood all nations of men for to dwell on all the face of the earth and hath determined the times before appointed and the bounds of their habitation, that they should seek the Lord, if haply they might feel after Him and find Him, though He be not far from every one of us; for in Him we live and move and have our being, as certain also of your own poets have said, 'For we are also His offspring.'" (Acts 17:22-28)

The statement is repeatedly made that there is no religion, crude or advanced, that has not in it the element of prayer. We are not well enough versed in the matter to ratify the statement. We do not know. But this we know, that the need for prayer and the desire to get in touch with the Highest is universal; for St. Paul says, "That they should seek the Lord, if haply they might feel after Him and find Him."

In one form or other, prayer is found everywhere, in all ages and among all people. The most discouraging circumstances do not crush it, and the most damaging "scientific" theories do not prevent it. Buddhism, theoretically a religion without a god, ought logically to exclude prayer because there is no higher being to be prayed to; yet in countries where Buddhism is dominant, prayer of a sort is practiced. Confucius, many of whose agnostic proverbs have gained favor, urged his disciples not to have much to do with gods; yet today Confucius himself is considered a god, and millions pray to him.

11

Climb the foothills of the Himalayas, visit the Khonds of Orissa, India, and you will hear the prayer: "O Lord, we know not what is good for us. Thou knowest what it is. For it we pray." Go back with the archaeologist to the Aztec ruins, and you will read this prayer in time of affliction: "O merciful Lord, let this chastisement with which Thou hast visited us give us freedom from evil and from folly." Study the history of ancient Greece, its conquests, its oratory, and its poetry. Xenophon began each day's march with prayer; Pericles began every address with prayer; Homer opened the *Iliad* with prayer. Its philosophers, too, spoke of prayer. Plato wrote, "Every man of sense before beginning an important work will ask help of the gods," and in practice he prayed, "King Zeus, grant us the good, whether we pray for it or not, but evil keep from us, though we pray for it." Epictetus wrote, "When thou hast shut thy door and darkened thy room, say not to thyself that thou art alone. God is in thy room."

Those who have visited Mohammedan strongholds not only have found formal prayer five times daily, when the muezzin calls from the minaret, but also have read descriptions of prayer like this from a Sufi, a Mohammedan mystic: "There are three degrees of prayer. The first is when it is only spoken by the lips. The second is when with difficulty, by resolute effort, the soul succeeds in fixing its thought on divine things. The third is when the soul finds it hard to turn away from God."

The Hebrew psalmist re-echoes the universal refrain: "O Thou that hearest prayer, unto Thee shall

all flesh come" (Psalm 65:2); and again, "The eyes of all wait upon Thee." (Psalm 145:15)

Why, then, if the instinct of prayer is universal and prayer a natural, necessary function of life, do we find people who do not pray? Because men stifle their capacity for worship, suppress the instinct of prayer, and pride themselves on their self-sufficiency. It is, indeed, quite possible to stifle the desire to pray. But in a desperate crisis even those who stifle the desire will be thrown back by that emergency upon the natural tendency to pray. The impulse to pray is exhibited in every human being — at least occasionally — suppress it though he may.

The instinctive turning of the heart to a power higher than man is felt not only in perilous crises but also under the weight of great responsibilities, for which a person unaided feels inadequate. Said Abraham Lincoln: "I have been driven many times to my knees by the overwhelming conviction that I had nowhere else to go; my own wisdom and that of all around me seemed insufficient for the day." Whenever a person faces tasks for which he feels inadequate and on the accomplishment of which much depends, he naturally turns to prayer; if he does not do so, he proves himself irrational and unnatural. (Cf. *Hear My Prayer*. London: Hodder and Stoughton)

A person, then, who squelches the urge to pray is blocking an elemental, natural function of human life — and proves himself a fool, for God's ordinance of prayer predicates the hunger of the soul of man for God. The desire for prayer is universal.

Especially do we Christians, the children of adoption, in whom the spirit of prayer has been reawakened by the Spirit of God, appreciate and acknowledge our need for prayer. "Prayer is absolutely essential for the Christian" (Constance Garrett, *Growth in Prayer,* p. 3). It is basic for his life. The only way the Christian can live a full-orbed and thoroughly furnished Christian life is by underlaying it with prayer; for prayer brings him into closer contact with Him whose power and Spirit undergird his life — even God. An electric light bulb, though properly manufactured, is of itself of little use except as an ornament. A wire must connect that bulb with the electrical impulses surging through the high line, before it can give off its glow — and even then the glow is not its own. So "prayer is the connecting cord" which brings us into closer contact with God and "which brings the power of God into our lives so that they can glow with a light" that is born of heaven. "My flesh and my heart faileth, but God is the Strength of my heart and my Portion forever. For, lo, they that are far from Thee shall perish; Thou hast destroyed all them that go a-whoring from Thee. But it is good for me to draw near to God; I have put my trust in the Lord God, that I may declare all Thy works." (Psalm 73:26-28)

We therefore pray because we have to pray. We can't get along without praying. We feel the same need to pray which Jesus felt when He withdrew into a mountainside. He could not do His work without prayer. Nor can we.

14

God's Ordinance of Prayer Gives an Insight into the Nature of Prayer

Prayer is thought of by some as nothing more than spiritual therapy. "Let a person pray in his distress, if he so desires. Even though there be no God who hears and answers prayer, even though God's laws are immutable and not subject to the caprice and whim of the pray-er, even though enlightened intellectuals recognize the utter foolishness of prayer, let a person pray in his distress, if he so desires. He will feel better after he gets his troubles off his chest; and even though no deity has been moved to action, he himself will feel stronger or relieved, as the case may be, because he has prayed. Why not take advantage of such spiritual therapy?"

This is far too limited a conception of prayer to do us much good.

PRAYER IS DESIRE

It means so much to us when we read: "Lord, Thou hast heard the desire of the humble" (Psalm 10:17). From it we learn that

> *Prayer is the soul's sincere desire,*
> *Unuttered or exprest,*
> *The motion of a hidden fire*
> *That trembles in the breast.*

(James Montgomery)

But not every desire is a prayer. The human heart is full of restless desires which continually search for an aspirinlike sedative. Indeed, these restless desires, often vain and contradictory, constitute one of the

15

great burdens of life. Wordsworth was right when he said,

> *Me this unchartered freedom tires;*
> *I feel the weight of chance desires.*

These restless "chance desires" may add to the need for prayer, but they are not yet prayers. To change these desires into prayers, we must first sift and correct them, regulate and restrain them, and bring them into harmony with the will of God. The desire must be the "desire of the humble," who are ready to confess: "Whom have I in heaven but Thee? And there is none upon earth that I desire beside Thee" (Psalm 73:25). Then the desire is good; then the desire is right; then the desire is God-pleasing; then the desire is a prayer.

A desire, then, to be a prayer, must be a Godward desire, reflecting the will of God and directed toward God. That the prayer of desire is and must be such a reflex of the divine will in the heart of the pray-er is expressly assumed in the words of Jesus: "What things soever ye desire, when ye pray, believe that ye receive them, and ye shall have them" (Mark 11:24); for here, surely, not every human desire is meant — whether of the juvenile delinquent who prays that he may not be caught, or of the aspiring son of a poor man who prays for success of a venture honorably undertaken, or "of suppliants all and sundry who pray for any boon which may make their lives more dignified, comfortable, and shadow-free" (James Hastings, *The Christian Doctrine of Prayer*, p. 29). Else every capricious human desire, good or bad, would

16

be the ultimate ruling force in nature — an inconsistent anomaly which the Lord Jesus never meant to suggest and which, when given the opportunity, He discouraged. You will recall the classic example of James and John, the sons of Zebedee. They came to Jesus with the request, "Master, we would that Thou shouldest do for us whatsoever we shall desire." But when Jesus ascertained the unreasonableness of their request — that one might sit on the right hand and the other on the left hand, in His glory — He told them, "Ye know not what ye ask" (Mark 10:35 ff.). Our desires must be channeled into the will of God, ready to serve the same purpose which all creation is meant to serve, namely, the glory of God. Then, we may rest assured, the desire of the humble will be heard by the Lord.

PRAYER IS PETITION

The ultramystic has a tendency to disparage petition and to call it "the lowest and crudest notion concerning prayer." That person, says the mystic, is hardly to be commended for his Christianity who is so self-centered as constantly to be plaguing the Lord of the universe with requests which to Him must be trivial. And yet, take the element of petition out of prayer, and prayer ceases to be what we mean by prayer or what the Savior had in mind when He spoke of the hungry child asking his father for bread or what St. Paul thought of as prayer when he instructed the Philippians to let their "requests be made known unto God."

17

For our own prayer life we must insist that petition, too, is prayer — in fact, that it is the elemental feature in prayer. With petition eliminated, there would be less praying than there is now; and we pray too little as it is. If our petitions, as some assert, were directed to a Supreme Being whose ear is deaf and whose heart is indifferent to our cries of distress and petitions for help; if this Supreme Being deigned to hear our prayer, but were unable to help us because of immutable laws which control both His action and our destiny, then, indeed, our petitioning would be no good. Prayer would be a mere academic question without practical value. We might as well then resign ourselves to the inevitable and, instead of spending fruitless time in prayer, endeavor to make the best of a condition of affairs for which there is no help but through our own ingenuity. If, however, we are assured that the heavenly Father, besides being pleased with our prayers of praise and thanksgiving, is willing to hear and does hear our petitions, then we shall be drawn to Him, knowing that our prayers and petitions are not in vain.

The assurance that our petitions are not in vain is borne out by Scripture both in precept and in example. By way of precept we have the many passages which bid us to ask, to seek, to pray. By way of example we may turn to Abraham, who interceded for Sodom; to Jacob, who wrestled all night with the Angel of the Lord, determined not to let Him go until He had granted his request for a blessing; to Moses, who by way of desperate prayer obtained mercy for his people; to Elijah, who sealed and unsealed the

18

heavens by prayer; and to the inspired poets who gave us the emotion-packed petitions of the Psalms. In the New Testament we have the examples of St. Paul, whose letters are flooded with petitions; of the prayer meetings recorded in the Acts of the Apostles; and of our Lord Jesus Himself, who spent whole nights in prayer upon a lonely mountainside, receiving strength from the heavenly Father for the work whereunto He had ordained Him.

PRAYER IS COMMUNION

Nonetheless prayer is more than desire and petition. Prayer is communion. Prayer is a talking to God, or better, a talking with God. Prayer is an intercommunion between ourselves and God. It is our response to God's invitation to come, the effort on our part to enter into that fellowship with God which He on His part desires to have with us and in which, as we pray, God would respond to us if only we would more often wait for a response. "To speak boldly," says Clement of Alexandria, "prayer is conversation and intercourse with God."

We Christians should want to talk with God. As we delight to speak with our friends, so we should be eager to speak with God, and, as we may say, "chat with Him as with a friend." Prayer should therefore never be a last-minute resort in the day of trouble but a daily habit. Every day there is something we should want to ask Him. Every day there is something we should want to tell Him. Every day there is something we should want to talk over with Him —

19

our thoughts, that we may receive His criticism or approval of them; our plans, that we may receive His advice. Every day we should want to express our affection, our admiration, our gratitude toward Him for His love and His friendship, to invite Him to share our joys, and to seek His sympathy in our sorrows. We Christians ought, indeed, be a praying people, daily communing with our God.

Prayer, since it is communion, cannot be a one-sided conversation. So often — too often — we make it so. We tell God all that we know (how infinitely little compared with His omniscience!), or we briefly inform Him about what is on our mind, and then we run off, never waiting for an answer or giving God an opportunity to respond to us. In prayer we should not insist on doing all the talking, nor should we run through our prayers almost without drawing a breath and then be done with them. We must in our prayers pause at times and give God a moment or two to talk with us and to respond to our prayer. We must give Him a chance to answer, whether that be in the form of reproof or comfort or instruction; whether it come as illumination to the mind or strength and courage to the heart. That is communion. That is completing the fellowship which God so greatly desires to have with us, His oft so wayward children.

Oh, the invitation of the Lord is so appealing and His promise so great! "If from thence thou shalt seek the Lord thy God, thou shalt find Him, if thou seek Him with all thy heart and with all thy soul. When thou art in tribulation and all these things are come upon thee, even in the latter days, if thou turn to the Lord thy God and shalt be obedient unto His voice — for the Lord thy God is a merciful God — He will not forsake thee neither destroy thee nor forget the covenant of thy fathers which He sware unto them" (Deuteronomy 4:29-31). Let's make haste to respond to the Lord's invitation! "When Thou saidst, Seek ye My face; my heart said unto Thee, Thy face, Lord, will I seek" (Psalm 27:8). God will respond — oh, yes, He will. "Draw nigh to God, and He will draw draw nigh to you." (James 4:8)

By way of example there comes to mind the experience of President William McKinley, when the problem of the future of the Philippine Islands was being considered. Said he in a subsequent public address: "I walked the floor of the White House night after night, and I am not ashamed to tell you, gentlemen, that I went down on my knees and prayed Almighty God for guidance more than one night. And one night late it came to me in this way. I don't know how it was, but it came. There was nothing left for us to do but to take them all, and to educate Filipinos and uplift and Christianize them, and by God's grace to do the very best we could for them as our fellow men for whom Christ died. And then I went to bed and went to sleep, and slept soundly." (Franklin Steiner, *The Religious Beliefs of Our Presidents.*)

If, then, prayer is communion between ourselves and God, in which we in response to His invitation come to Him and He in response to our appeal comes to us, then it follows that God's ordinance of prayer

21

also assures us of the fact that our prayers are "accept-able to our Father in heaven and are heard by Him; for He Himself has commanded us so to pray and has promised to hear us."

God's ordinance of prayer takes for granted the guarantee that our prayer, when it meets the neces-sary requirements, is acceptable and heard. "This is the confidence that we have in Him," writes St. John, "that if we ask anything according to His will, He heareth us." (1 John 5:14)

GOD'S PROMISES TO THIS EFFECT

There are many reasons for believing that God answers prayer. But for a Christian the best reason is that God says so in the Bible.

Hear the Word of the Lord! Its ironclad promises will amaze you if you but pause to analyze and to evaluate them!

"Lord, Thou hast heard the desire of the humble; Thou wilt prepare their heart, Thou wilt cause Thine ear to hear." (Psalm 10:17)

"Call upon Me in the day of trouble, I will deliver thee." (Psalm 50:15)

"O Thou that hearest prayer, unto Thee shall all flesh come." (Psalm 65:2)

"He shall call upon Me, and I will answer him; I will be with him in trouble; I will deliver him and

22

honor him. With long life will I satisfy him and show him My salvation." (Psalm 91:15, 16)

"And it shall come to pass that before they call I will answer; and while they are yet speaking, I will hear." (Isaiah 65:24)

"Pray to thy Father which is in secret, and thy Father which seeth in secret shall reward thee openly." (Matthew 6:6)

"When ye pray, use not vain repetitions, as the heathen do; for they think that they shall be heard for their much speaking. Be not ye therefore like unto them; for your Father knoweth what things ye have need of, before ye ask Him." (Matthew 6:7, 8)

"Ask, and it shall be given you; seek, and ye shall find; knock, and it shall be opened unto you." (Matthew 7:7)

"All things whatsoever ye shall ask in prayer, believing, ye shall receive." (Matthew 21:22)

"What things soever ye desire, when ye pray, believe that ye receive them, and ye shall have them." (Mark 11:24)

"If ye abide in Me, and My words abide in you, ye shall ask what ye will, and it shall be done unto you." (John 15:7)

"Whatsoever ye shall ask the Father in My name, He will give it you." (John 16:23)

"The effectual fervent prayer of a righteous man availeth much." (James 5:16)

"This is the confidence that we have in Him, that if we ask anything according to His will, He heareth us." (1 John 5:14)

"These promises" — so writes C. A. Behnke in an essay on "Prayer" in *The Abiding Word* (I, 252) — "these promises, marvelous in character and scope, have as their Guarantor Him of whom the Bible says (Hebrews 10:23b): 'He is faithful that promised. . . .'

"Add to this the consideration that these promises are an integral part of a covenant, a contract, of which God Himself assures us (Isaiah 54:10): 'The mountains shall depart and the hills be removed; but My kindness shall not depart from thee, neither shall the covenant of My peace be removed, saith the Lord that hath mercy on thee.'

"In the midst of these covenant-supported promises the inspired apostle Paul places the Cross as the supreme guarantee when he writes (Romans 8:32): 'He that spared not His own Son but delivered Him up for us all, how shall He not with Him also freely give us all things?' What does that mean? Nothing less than this, that God in His infinite love has already presented the greatest gift in His possession, Him who was nearest and dearest to Him, His only-begotten Son. All that we have a right to expect on the basis of the promises made for this life and that which is to come is small in comparison with what we have already received.

"Can God do more to assure us?"

We who have been led by the Spirit of God to the hill of Calvary, what reason have we to doubt the promises of God? For in Him, whose sacrifice inspired the crucifix — "all the promises of God in Him are yea, and in Him Amen" (2 Corinthians 1:20). "Amen, Amen, that is, Yea, yea, it shall be so."

Now notice and appreciate once again the loving concern of the heavenly Father. "Like as a father pitieth his children, so the Lord pitieth them that fear Him. For He knoweth our frame; He remembereth that we are dust" (Psalm 103:13, 14); and because He knows, He has given us sample upon sample of how He has answered prayer.

Take the case of Elijah, who was a man of like nature as we are. He prayed fervently that it might not rain, and for three years and six months, in judgment against the wickedness of King Ahab, it did not rain in Israel. Then he prayed again, and the heaven gave rain, and the earth brought forth its fruit (James 5:17, 18). Later, when confronted with the prophets of Baal, he prayed, and fire came from heaven and ignited the water-soaked sacrifice after the prophets of Baal amidst flagellations and slashings had called in vain upon their idol.

Take the case of King Hezekiah. He was sick, at the very point of death. He prayed, "and his life was extended fifteen years."

Take the case of aged Zacharias, the father of John the Baptizer. The angel told him, "Thy prayer is heard; and thy wife, Elizabeth, shall bear thee a son." (Luke 1:13)

Take the case of Paul and Silas. At Philippi they were imprisoned for preaching the Gospel of Christ. They prayed, and an earthquake shook the prison, and barred gates were unloosed.

25

Are these examples too remote?

Some of you who read these words have been sick — sick unto death, and you prayed, and your parents and your pastor and your friends prayed — and today you are well.

I knew a lad who in the tender years of his childhood was puny and not at all well. So often was he face to face with death that he dreaded even to close his eyes in sleep. It was not that he was afraid of death; but he dreaded the repeated agony of it — a-dying and never dead. For six long years — and to a child six years are mighty long — for six long years he yearned and sighed and prayed. This little boy had a Christian mother who in her love for him was deeply concerned. She prayed as only a tortured mother heart can pray; and in her prayer she promised the Lord that, if He but restore her boy to health, he in turn should be dedicated to the service of the Lord. In time for the mother to keep her promise the lad was restored to health and has not been seriously ill since. Today he is in the ministry, dedicated to the Lord by his now sainted mother.

When this same lad, still as a young man, was attending the seminary, there came to him a letter from his mother informing him that his brother was desperately sick and that the doctor had given him but eight hours to live. That night he knelt at his bed, and over the miles traveled an effectual prayer. His brother sank, he hovered in the crisis — and passed it. Indeed, he had already passed the crisis, even before the letter had reached the brother, but the brother who that night prayed for him has always believed that God heard and answered his prayer, according to His promise: "It shall come to pass that before they call, I will answer; and while they are yet speaking, I will hear." (Isaiah 65:24)

Several years later this same young man, who had already experienced the faithfulness of a prayer-answering God, saw the wife of his youth wheeled into an operating room for a serious operation. His prayers, though incoherent and inarticulate to anyone but God, were fervent and desperate. A little son of a year and a half needed that mother. Back through the door of the operating room was wheeled the young mother, her heartbeat weak, her life hovering very near to eternity. Fervent prayers hung on to that slender thread. The mother rallied. She mended. She lived — to lead to God the sons of the man who so fervently prayed that her life be spared.

But in all fairness to the subject under consideration, and in all fairness to God, who has given us the holy privilege of prayer, let us leave the realm of striking and spectacular answers to prayer and give a little consideration to ordinary answers. There is that simplest of all simple prayers, "Give us this day our daily bread." For at least forty-six years we have prayed that simple prayer, and for fifty-one years the Lord has never ceased to answer it. And His ordinary answer to that simple prayer is as miraculous as the answers which to us appear more spectacular! Where lies the difference?

Contend that God willed in the first place to do things just as they did happen, that God anticipated the prayers and therefore worked it just so; we grant that this is so and rejoice over it. Of course God, who lives in timeless eternity, anticipates our prayers, for He knows even our thoughts afar off; but here is our comfort: because He does anticipate, He is able to arrange matters so that He may answer our prayers. It's in the very nature of God's ordinance of prayer that our prayers, when they meet the necessary requirements, are acceptable to God and heard by Him. His ordinance of prayer does therefore, indeed, guarantee an answer to prayer, "for the word of the Lord is right, and all His works are done in truth." (Psalm 33:4)

2.

Difficulties in the Way of Prayer

For one who has learned to trust God and upon His mere word to launch out into the deep, prayer needs no justification. It justifies itself, just as breathing justifies itself. We breathe — and live. Were we to cease to breathe, we would cease to live. Our life is proof sufficient of the value of breathing and of its efficacy. Similarly we pray — and live to God. Were we to cease to pray, we would cease to live to God. Our Christian life is proof sufficient of the value of prayer and of its efficacy.

And yet difficulties of the intellect have grown up around prayer, perplexing and chilling the hearts of many. Prayer is unscientific and ineffectual, we are told. Prayer is superfluous and impertinent. Prayer is superstitious and foolish. What we suppose to be answers to our prayers can all be explained away by simply using elementary logic.

It seems, then, that for the sake of the pray-er prayer does need to be justified. At least it would greatly assist us in our prayer life, if the difficulties in the way of prayer were removed.

SCIENTIFIC DIFFICULTIES

Let us tackle the most baffling difficulty first — the assertion that prayer is unscientific and therefore quite ineffectual.

The claim is made that an answer to prayer would involve the interruption of the established order in the universe. God has established certain laws by which He governs the universe. These laws are fixed and immutable. Prayer therefore seeks the unattainable; it demands a result which is opposed to the whole order and course of the universe!

When you pray, expecting an answer, says the objector, you are asking God to bring about for you something which would not otherwise happen, to change by direct intervention the regular sequence of events — in plain words, to work a miracle in your behalf. This is more than mere man has a right to expect, that he by his prayer can prevail upon the Omnipotent to sidetrack the great through traffic of the universe in order to give his local train the right of way. How can we believe it possible that the majestic universe should be ruled in this fitful way, by arbitrary miraculous interferences, at every whim and demand of thousands of selfish petitioners? It is inconsistent with what we know of the laws of nature and of the nature of God. A miracle is impossible in a universe governed and controlled by fixed laws.

Furthermore, even if a miracle were possible, how can we expect God to violate the laws which He Himself has established and fixed, in order to show us a special favor, or to supply our want, or to gratify our desire? The universe is not ruled by such caprice. Time was, and that but recently, when it was pardonable that men should pray for rain or for fair weather, for health or abundant harvests; but in this scientific age it is no longer rational for us to do so.

In our scientifically enlightened age darkness has given place to light, confusion has given place to order, and caprice has give place to law; and we can no longer believe that by our prayers we are able to change the supreme will which works out the welfare of the universe according to laws which are as fixed and unchangeable as the Supreme Being Himself, so much so that He, who is supreme, is Himself bound by them.

We know that rain is the product of atmospheric laws which under certain conditions render it impossible or inevitable, as the case may be, and that it is therefore unreasonable to expect God to supply on our immediate demand what could not be provided but by previous evaporation.

We know that health or disease are the result of physiological laws which absolutely determine that one man shall live and another die and that it is therefore unreasonable and even unnecessary to ask God to intervene when our doctors have a supply of won-

31

der drugs which upon application will produce the necessary chemical reaction that will arrest the disease and restore health. (Cf. Hastings, pp. 220 ff.)

These "scientific" objections are replete with unscientific conceptions.

The basic conception of all these so-called scientific objections to the efficacy of prayer is that this world is governed by certain fixed and invariable laws — immutable and unchangeable.

Nothing is more unscientific than such a statement. Law in itself has no governing power. The world we live in is not ruled *by* certain laws, it is ruled *according to* certain laws. Every game has rules, but the game is not played by the rules; the players play the game according to the rules. And so the world in which we live is not governed by certain laws, but according to certain laws; and He who governs it is God, the Omnipotent. The laws of nature are, after all, nothing more than God's will in operation.

If, now, we believe God to be fettered in His governance by the laws which He ordinarily observes, then we raise abstract law and order above God; we place God in a category lower than His creation; we cease to believe in God. God governs according to laws, but is not Himself governed by laws; nor is this universe governed by laws; it is governed by God according to certain laws. All this may sound profound. It simply means this, that fundamentally these laws are nothing more or less than the observed regularity with which God works in nature. If, then, He works in nature at all, if He controls the universe according to laws which He Himself has established, can it be illogical to ask Him to hold His hand or to hasten His work? Since His actions have determined the laws, the laws are powerless to fetter His actions.

He to whom we pray may therefore be trusted to grant our prayer or to refuse it, as may seem best to His highest wisdom and truest love. And if He chooses to grant our prayer, He certainly does not lack the necessary resources to make it possible, even though to do so might mean that He suspend what we call a natural law. This is in line with what we know of God, who "is able to do exceeding abundantly above all that we ask or think" (Ephesians 3:20) and in whose will every phenomenon of nature has its creative cause.

The laws of nature established by God are immutable only insofar as God wills them to be immutable. But what of the will of God? Is it immutable so that we cannot possibly influence it by our feeble prayers? To answer this question in the affirmative would mean to make God a captive of His own will and a fatalistic automaton.

If God has any will — and He has — it must remain free, or God would not be God. And that God's will is not always predetermined and permanently set and He a captive of His own device, we see from the incident of King Hezekiah's recovery, when upon his prayer the Lord added fifteen years to his life even after having announced to him, "Set thine house in order; for thou shalt die, and not live" (2 Kings 20), or from the even more striking incident of Joash, king of Israel, who at the behest of Elisha smote the ground but three times with his arrows, when by smiting the

33

ground five or six times he could have assured himself a complete and decisive victory over Syria (2 Kings 13:14-19). In the one instance there was a change in God's will; in the other there was a choice. Both change and choice spell freedom of will. God's will is free — free to act as He will, free also to be influenced by our prayers.

Jesus was never concerned about scientific difficulties in the way of prayer. He spoke of difficulties — lack of faith, lack of perseverance, difficulties on man's side — but scientific difficulties were never among them. He who was in the bosom of the Father knew that with God nothing is impossible and that the rules of His actions are not limited to the broad uniformities which we call the laws of nature.

Or must we, in order to remain scientific, think of God as being able to do less than man?

When God created Adam, He gave him "dominion over the fish of the sea and over the fowl of the air and over every living thing that moveth upon the earth" (Genesis 1:28). From that day on much of the work of the world has been done by natural forces under human guidance. This work is the outcome of a combination of the laws of nature and of the purpose of man. All our wonderful inventions, the wheel, the lever, the steam engine, the hydraulic press, the telegraph, the telephone, the generator, the radio, television, even the atom bomb, are nothing less than the will of man restraining, combining, directing, and utilizing the law-observing forces of nature. Man is able to make the laws of nature serve his purpose without violating these laws.

34

So also God can and does use His knowledge of the natural laws to help us in answer to our prayers, especially when we have exhausted all our efforts and no longer know what to do. After all, He has a better grasp of the science of natural laws than we, and for Him to suspend is as easy as to establish. He has the immense reservoir of omniscience and omnipotence to draw from. Extremities are no deterrent to Him as they are to us. In fact, there are for Him no extremities.

We may be perplexed with heartbreaking problems which torture us day and night and which clamor for solution but baffle us with continuing frustration. These are the very things to bring to the Lord, whose eyes penetrate to all the secret mysteries of life. Why not follow the reasoning of the Lord Jesus? A father can use his knowledge of natural laws for his child without violating those laws. "If ye, then, being evil, know how to give good gifts unto your children, how much more shall your heavenly Father give the Holy Spirit to them that ask Him?" (Luke 11:13)

And lest anybody try to limit the ability of the heavenly Father to granting only requests for spiritual blessings, and so fall into the error of Schleiermacher and others who "divided the world of reality into two great departments or realms — the realm of the external, physical nature," which, they say, is governed by immutable law, "and the realm of the soul," in which God is free to act with greater liberty, let him keep in mind that "He that spared not His own Son but delivered Him up for us all, how shall He not with Him also freely give us all things?" (Romans 8:32).

Certainly He who found the key to open heaven can by His will release the forces of nature to suit His own purpose; and if He permits that purpose to be influenced by our prayers, shall we permit any scientific considerations to keep us from praying?

PHILOSOPHIC DIFFICULTIES

Other objections to the efficacy of prayer, indeed, even to the necessity of prayer, may be called philosophic difficulties.

THE PERFECT PROVIDENCE OF GOD

Chief of these is the perfect providence of God. In His loving concern Jesus tells us, "Your heavenly Father knoweth that ye have need of all these things" (Matthew 6:32); and the prayer-skeptic concludes, "Then why should we ask?"

The argument behind this objection is to the effect that the perfect providence of God makes prayer superfluous. God knows everything and will do what is best for us and for everyone without our asking. The Omniscient One need not be informed of what we need and as to how we feel. Why act as if He were ignorant and pour into His ear what to Him must be a tedious catalog of wants and desires? He has heard all that before, and He knew it was coming.

For a child of God this is a strange argument, for next to the redeeming love of God there is hardly another quality in God that is so attractive as His providential love. The perfect providence of God does not repel the child of God; it attracts him, it draws him.

The child of God prays because he believes so strongly in the perfect providence of God; he prays because he believes that all things, even his wants and desires, are known to God; for if they were not, what assurance would he — could he — have that his petitions ever reached the ear of God at all? Far more reasonable to reverse the argument and say, "If God did not know everything, what would be the use of praying?" This is the argument which Jesus uses. "When ye pray, use not vain repetitions, as the heathen do; for they think that they shall be heard for their much speaking. Be not ye therefore like unto them; for your Father knoweth what things ye have need of before ye ask Him" (Matthew 6:7, 8). God knows all, therefore no vain repetitions are necessary; but prayer itself is nonetheless encouraged. What a strange family where the parents' knowledge of the children's needs would fetter their tongues for requests!

Another argument which in this connection is meant to discourage prayer makes of prayer an impertinent intrusion, an attempt to bend the will of God to our own will, to make God swerve from the course which His perfect wisdom has outlined, and to suit His actions to our private inclinations. "How can any sensible, right-minded person be guilty of such effrontery? If your desires are right, God naturally will grant them; if they are wrong, they do not deserve to be granted, and you should be ashamed of trying to make God bend to your will. So, in either case prayer is either superfluous or impertinent."

Answer: A Christian would not want to be impertinent in his prayers; and because he does not want to be impertinent, he prays. He does not demand, for a demand would be impertinent.

But pray he does; and at times he will storm the very gate of heaven with his prayers and beat the bosom of the Father in his great need. Is that effrontery? If the Son of God tells me, "Ask, and it shall be given you; seek, and ye shall find; knock, and it shall be opened unto you" (Matthew 7:7), and so encourages me to confront God with prayer, then my prayers, even when in their fervency they border on impertinence, cannot be termed effrontery. Why be so concerned about tiring and wearying a resourceful Father with our prayers? We are not praying to an incomprehensible abstraction whose providence is limited by our comprehension. We are praying to a gracious, loving, sympathizing, condescending God who delights in our troublesome persistency.

Luther has a wonderful answer for those who would make of the perfect providence of God a difficulty in the way of prayer. "God gives daily bread indeed without our prayer, also to all the wicked; but we pray in this petition that He would lead us to know it and to receive our daily bread with thanksgiving."

THE INSIGNIFICANCE OF MAN

We come now to a philosophic difficulty in the way of prayer which without thorough thought might appeal to the humility which is so characteristic of a prayerful heart. We have in mind the insignificance of man.

"O Lord, our Lord, how excellent is Thy name in all the earth! who hast set Thy glory above the heavens. . . . When I consider Thy heavens, the work of Thy fingers, the moon and the stars, which Thou hast ordained, what is man that Thou art mindful of him? and the son of man that Thou visitest him?" (Psalm 8:1-4). The thought is overwhelming! over-powering in its pathos!

Through the telescope we peer into space that appears illimitable. Our world seems so large, yet 93,000,000 miles away, hung in space, is the sun, many hundred times bigger than the world on which we live. The world is dwarfed. And yet how close, how very close to the earth is the sun — only eight light-minutes away. Beyond the sun are the stars, of which on a clear night some five thousand are visible to the naked eye, over two million through a small telescope, and billions through the great Palomar telescope. Of all these stars, the nearest to our earth, save the sun, is the star Alpha Centauri, which is four and four-tenths light-years away. (A light-year is the distance light travels in a year, roughly six trillion miles.) Betelgeuse, the variable red giant star of the first magnitude in the shoulder of Orion, is 300 light-years away. The light from Rigel, the blue giant of the first magnitude in the left foot of the constellation Orion, takes 540 years to reach our eyes. "When I consider Thy heavens, the work of Thy fingers, the moon and the stars, which Thou hast ordained" — the earth is dwarfed to an infinitesimal speck — "what is man —?"

And above the heavens is set the glory of God! I as man, *Enosh,* frail, mortal man; I as man, *Ben-*

39

Adam, son of Adam and of the earth, inhabitant of a speck already infinitesimally small, should dare to expect individual attention from Him who has created and who sustains a creation that is unreachable in its vastness? The thought is overpowering. And as it overpowers me, it is only natural that I should feel awed, timid, and hesitant in bringing my needs to the attention of the Most High!

But think! Think as a child of God. "What is man that Thou art mindful of him?" asks David, and then proceeds to answer his own question: "Thou hast made him a little lower than the angels and hast crowned him with glory and honor. Thou madest him to have dominion over the works of Thy hands; Thou hast put all things under his feet" (Psalm 8:5, 6). Of all the creatures great or small, vast or limited, man, as the crown of God's creation, is yet the chief object of His concern. "Are not two sparrows sold for a farthing? And one of them shall not fall on the ground without your Father. But the very hairs of your head are all numbered" (Matthew 10:29, 30). Why, then, our timid hesitancy? We may not be able to conceive how God, weigh and sift as He must the unnumbered petitions which rise to Him in prayer, can attend to our individual care, but we know that He does. His knowledge is both broad and detailed. "The Lord doth build up Jerusalem; He gathereth together the outcasts of Israel. He healeth the broken in heart and bindeth up their wounds. He telleth the number of the stars; He calleth them all by their names. Great is our Lord and of great power; His understanding is infinite." (Psalm 147:2-5)

40

Think again. The One to whom we pray and before whom the inhabitants of the world are asked to stand in awe (Psalm 33:8), "was made flesh and dwelt among us, and we beheld His glory, the glory as of the Only-begotten of the Father, full of grace and truth" (John 1:14). He became man — one of us. He also was wounded and was hungry and cold. He was betrayed by a friend, forsaken by His disciples, and murdered by those whom He came to help. He is sensitive to our need and sympathetic. "Seeing, then, that we have a great High Priest, that is passed into the heavens, Jesus, the Son of God, let us hold fast our profession. For we have not an high priest which cannot be touched with the feeling of our infirmities, but was in all points tempted like as we are, yet without sin. Let us therefore come boldly unto the throne of grace that we may obtain mercy and find grace to help in time of need." (Hebrews 4:14-16)

Think again. "Our Father, who art in heaven." So Jesus teaches us to address the almighty Creator and Sustainer of heaven and earth. "God would by these words tenderly invite us to believe that He is our true Father and that we are His true children, so that we may with all boldness and confidence ask Him as dear children ask their dear father."

Insignificant? Yes. — Forgotten, forsaken, neglected? No!

CONFLICTING INTERESTS

Philosophic difficulties and objections are easy to come by if we look for them — too easy for our own good.

41

One difficulty which by many is deemed almost insurmountable is the difficulty of conflicting interests. One man or one people may ask for that which would be injurious to another. The Germans, that is, those among them who believed in God and in prayer, prayed for the success of their panzer divisions; the Allies, that is, those among them who believed in a God higher than themselves and more powerful than their munitions, prayed for the success of their combined efforts. How could God answer the prayer of both sides or even of either side? In this case we like to believe that "God gave victory to the side which was right." This answer does not satisfy, for on the side of victory were sinners as black as and blacker than the vanquished. Furthermore, there have been instances when victory did not go to the just.

The problem of conflicting interests appears, indeed, to be insurmountable until we keep in mind that every Christian prayer for specific temporal blessings is tacitly, if not expressly, conditioned; and the condition is this: "Nevertheless, not my will, but Thine, be done." Whatever the Christian may pray for, whether it be victory in a battle, restoration of health, change of weather, personal advancement, success of a venture, he deliberately requests that his prayer should be refused if to grant it would mean a contravention of God's will. There will be no conflict.

THE CHARGE OF SUPERSTITION

Let us consider another philosophic difficulty in the way of prayer. It is the charge that prayer is superstitious. It is held that statistics prove prayer quite ineffectual, for it is not found to have had any results in the over-all picture or to have made any observable difference in the course of events.

For instance (and these arguments are meant to clinch the point), in Christian states there are no persons more consistently prayed for than monarchs or rulers, "both that they may live long and that they may be endowed with wisdom and virtue"; yet this fact does not seem to have prolonged their lives beyond the average; nor have they always been conspicuous for moral superiority. In spite of the prayers of the faithful they have often made a thorough mess of things.

Again, it is pointed out that children of Christian parents are prayed for constantly, yet they do not appear to be free from sickness or accidents, nor do they live longer, nor are they more prosperous. Praying soldiers are not exempt from death in battle. Praying farmers harvest no better crops, and devout merchants have no better markets, than their prayerless neighbors.

Where does this leave us? We answer in quiet resignation: "Thy will be done," and join Job in flinging out the challenge: "Though He slay me, yet will I trust in Him" (Job 13:15). To the charge itself we answer: "You have appealed to experience, and to experience we shall go. Only let it be Christian experience." Wherever there has been a praying Christian, there has been a believer in the efficacy of prayer; and to a man of faith, who with his faith has coupled experience, you just can't talk the way you do. He has prayed, and he has received answers to his prayers;

and the argument that statistics "disprove" his experience does not give him any concern. He has no doubts about it; he knows that God answers his prayers; and what the outside world is quick to call failure of prayer is to him no failure but God's way of answering his prayer. For his soul's wants he continues to storm the gate of heaven with a force to which God gladly yields; for temporal help he continues to ask but does not trouble to tabulate the results, although results there are aplenty.

Experimental Difficulties

We have appealed to experience, but experience, too, craves an answer; for there is also such a thing as an experimental difficulty in the way of prayer.

Jesus says, "Men ought always to pray, and not to faint" (Luke 18:1). So intensely did He desire His disciples to believe it and to practice it that He told them a parable to fix it in their minds. This is the parable of the Unscrupulous Judge and the Importunate Widow; and the point of the parable is that here was prayer whose very persistence brought deliverance. "But" somebody may feel, "that is not my experience. I feel at times the apparent failure and uselessness of prayer because nothing seems to happen. I pray and pray, and the answer does not come. The life is not saved. The burden is not lifted. The sorrow remains as deep as ever. I am tempted to believe that nobody hears my prayers but me." I suppose that every one of us has had a similar experience. We have left the sickroom or the hospital or the place

44

of business or the broken home or the tragedy-ridden family, feeling that the world is empty and that we cry aloud when there is no answer but the echo of our own cry.

I should like to pass on to you John Bunyan's words when he was burdened with this same problem. He had been reading this parable of the Importunate Widow and took it as a direct message from God to his soul to encourage him to pray. And how he needed that encouragement! These are his words: "The tempter laid again at me very sore, suggesting that neither the mercy of God nor yet the blood of Christ did at all concern me, nor could they help me for my sin; therefore it was vain to pray. Yet, thought I, I will pray. 'But,' said the tempter, 'your sin is unpardonable.' 'Well,' said I, 'I will pray.' 'It is to no boot,' said he. 'Yet,' said I, 'I will pray.' So I went to prayer and while at prayer uttered these words: 'Lord, Satan tells me that neither Thy mercy nor the blood of Christ is sufficient to save my soul. Lord, shall I honor Thee most by believing that Thou wilt and canst, or him, by believing that Thou neither wilt nor canst? Lord, I would fain honor Thee by believing that Thou wilt and canst.'"

In our doubts about the efficacy of prayer we shall do well to copy John Bunyan in that spirit of perseverance. In the face of all that would deter and discourage us, let us say, "Yet I will pray!" The best way to overcome this difficulty in the way of prayer is to pray.

Furthermore, let us keep in mind that sometimes our heavenly Father has to answer our prayer with "no." He did it in the case of St. Paul. He did it in the case of Jesus Christ, His own Son. St. Paul asked that his burden, the thorn in the flesh, be removed, and it was not. At first he apparently received no answer, and in time the only answer that came back to him was: "My grace is sufficient for thee; for My strength is made perfect in weakness" (2 Corinthians 12:9). That, too, was an answer, the best that could be given. Jesus, before him, had the same experience, and to it we return again and again when we think of our seemingly unanswered prayers. In the Garden of Gethsemane He prayed three times the same agonizing prayer: "If it be possible, let this cup pass from Me." The cup did not pass from Him but instead was pressed to His lips, and He was compelled to drink it to the very bottom. Nevertheless, He kept on praying, for through prayer He knew that He would receive the divine energy which was necessary for the accomplishment of God's purpose in the cup which He had given His Son to drink. In answer to His prayer "there appeared an angel unto Him from heaven, strengthening Him." (Luke 22:43)

Sometimes our heavenly Father answers also our prayers with "no." After all, our prayers cannot always result in things coming our way. They must always be the victory of God's way, if necessary through us. But God always answers, even if not always according to our wishes.

Some people who have had little instruction in prayer and who have given the subject little thought seem to think that God is obliged, because of His promise, to give them anything and everything they might ask for. That guarantee is not contained in the Lord's promise; for He cannot do that, and He will not do it. God does, indeed, through His apostle Paul urge us, "In everything by prayer and supplication with thanksgiving let your requests be made known unto God" (Philippians 4:6); but God takes for granted that we, being His children, will not deliberately ask for things that would embarrass Him or injure us; and we take for granted that He, being our Father, will sift the harmful from the good in our petitions and give us only "good things" (Matthew 7:11). This reservation God must make if we are not to lose confidence in His continued goodness. To be able to retain that confidence, we must have the assurance that He is more careful in the granting of our requests than we are in the asking of them. It is in the very nature of His goodness that it should be so. We can, therefore, pray with complete confidence in God's wisdom, knowing that His answer to our prayers will never harm us.

You see, God's wisdom, like His love, is long-term wisdom. It has the sweep of years in it and all the reaches of eternity. Every prayer we pray is heard by God and is answered by Him, often by an overwhelming "yes" far beyond our expectation; but sometimes it is "no." Sometimes God's answer must be "no" for the present because His long-term wisdom foresees the harm which a "yes" might cause.

We speak too soon when we complain. Someday we shall be surprised to count the number of our answered prayers.

You may think of other difficulties in the way of prayer.

You may want to plead inexperience, saying, "I really do not know how to pray." Perhaps you are praying in a manner that is not at all adapted to you. Remember David trying on the armor of Saul. It was too large, too heavy, too cumbersome — unaccustomed. Are you making the same mistake? Are you trying to pray as the minister does and use the language he uses in prayer? It may be too heavy for you. You may have to do as David did: go back to the sling, the simplest of all weapons, and be content to pray as a child. Use monosyllabic prayers, simple prayers. Simple prayers are so much easier to pray. You need not try to make what you might call a "good" prayer, well rounded out and collected. Be satisfied with what you think a "poor" prayer. Never mind the language, never mind how the prayer begins or how it ends, just pray. Let your feelings burst out. A prayer from a burdened heart may be in a single sentence. "Oh, help me, good Lord!" Even an interjection is a prayer. A sigh is a prayer. Greater minds may elaborate the prayer, but they can make it no more fervent nor more effectual, for the fervency of the prayer depends not on its length or brevity or on its composition and diction but on the heart that prays it.

THE WANDERING MIND

Another difficulty that faces us in prayer is the wandering mind. I suppose we have all experienced

48

the weakness that only too often, as we pray, our minds go off to the ends of the earth while we say words and phrases and repeat expressions which we mean should convey our thoughts. "We are like little children saying our prayers and letting our thoughts run riot through all the play experiences of the day."

Now, it is a human failing that with the majority of us the power of concentration is limited; and it is very difficult for us to concentrate over a longer period of time — even also in prayer. The wandering thoughts willy-nilly "keep straying away and will not fasten on the prayer" that we are praying. What shall we do to correct the failing? Try harder. Keep at it. Start again. Pray the prayer over and over till the prayer is prayed through without a wandering thought. And if you cannot, then confess, and ask the Lord to help.

However, there do come times when the thoughts are utterly exhausted — times, too, that call for prayer more than others; and the weary thoughts refuse to accompany the prayer. At such times be satisfied with short prayers. Say only as much as you have to say. The publican, when he prayed in the temple, "God, be merciful to me, a sinner," had no trouble with wandering thoughts. But had he tried to prolong his prayer, his thoughts might have begun to wander.

Even so, the fact remains that some just do not have the power of concentration. Let them, by all means, be brief. Said Savonarola, an Italian reformer of the fifteenth century (A. D. 1452–1498), "Seeing that, when in this matter we make a beginning, it is not possible for us to maintain attention for long, it

49

is a good thing to pray briefly and often, and that with much attention and devotion" (A. J. Gossip, *In the Secret Place of the Most High,* p. 50). And our Lord, who spent whole nights in prayer, understanding the weakness of His disciples, gave them a comprehensive prayer which can be prayed in a matter of seconds — less than one minute — without doing it violence, saying to them: "When ye pray, say: Our Father which art in heaven, hallowed be Thy name. Thy kingdom come. Thy will be done, as in heaven, so in earth. Give us day by day our daily bread. And forgive us our sins; for we also forgive every one that is indebted to us. And lead us not into temptation; but deliver us from evil." (Luke 11:2-4)

PHYSICAL WEAKNESS

A failing common to us all is our physical weakness. We are tired; we are overworked; we are weary; we are sick, or none too fit, or the like. What pastor hasn't heard the complaint rise from a haggard face, "Pastor, I cannot pray"? Often, what the patient means is that in his sickness and in his fever-weakened condition he cannot recall the prayers he once memorized or that he cannot get beyond the introductory line. He is deeply concerned about it. "Pastor, I cannot pray."

"I believe in God — God the almighty Maker of heaven and earth?" Yes, surely. But more to the point just now is the confession, "I believe in God the Father." Every reasonable parent makes allowances for weaknesses in a child and, quickly diagnosing what is the matter, is doubly kind and patient if he but senses that the heart is right. And the loving Father of us all, remembering that we are but dust, and delighting in mercy, is divinely understanding.

"Pastor, I cannot pray." What would Jesus say to ease his troubled heart? "When you pray, say, Our Father." If you can't remember the prayers you once memorized, just tell the heavenly Father what is on your mind. "O Father, I am in pain, relieve me"; or, "Dear Father in heaven, forgive me my sins for Jesus' sake"; or, "Heavenly Father, give your beloved sleep"; or, "Father, Abba Father, I cannot pray. Help me!" Remember, you are praying to a generous God, to a loving God, to One who loves you better than you can love yourself, to One who would fain take you up in His arms, while you are praying, and help you. And help you He will. He will send you His Holy Spirit to assist you in prayer or, if you are utterly too weak, to pray for you. "Likewise the Spirit helps us in our weakness; for we do not know how to pray as we ought, but the Spirit himself intercedes for us with sighs too deep for words." (Romans 8:26 RSV)

THE ELEMENT OF TIME

Whatever difficulties there may be in the way of prayer, let's not — you and me — let's never plead the time element. "We know quite well that our prayer life is a meager affair, thin and stunted." We hold too little communion with God between wakening in the morning and falling asleep at night. The road of prayer, "once so frequented, has become lonely

51

and neglected and grass-grown." We do not walk it often enough. And when we do strike the road in our earthly travels, we all too soon and all too frequently detour. Hurried and perfunctory prayers have become our plague. It isn't that we like it that way. It isn't that we want it that way. It isn't that we are satisfied that way. We all intend to pray more than we do; but the press of life, the demands of the hour, the unexpected interruptions interfere with our good intentions — and we forget — and we neglect. Oh, but things must not interfere! And we must not neglect! Our supreme need is to learn to worship and to pray, really to live and move and have our being in God. To learn, we just cannot let things drift, we must do something about our prayer life.

Prayer is an art. If we wish to learn the art of prayer or learn it better, it seems apparent — does it not? — that we must be prepared to spare such time and to take such pains, and more, as we give to the learning of any other art which we think means much for our life.

Counselors to Encourage Us

And why should we be so listless in prayer, so slow to venture out into the deepest possible depths of prayer, when God has given us two well-accredited attorneys to encourage us?

C. E. Brown, in *The Way of Prayer* (p. 139), states that in the British system of law there are, or were, two kinds of lawyers for the client, one who advises him privately as to what course to pursue in his defense and another who represents him in court. The one who represents him in court must be of the highest character, and the other no less.

Now without reflecting on the character of the other Advocate (for I shrink from the thought of blaspheming Him), the Counsel who represents us in prayer at the court of God is of the highest character. It is Jesus Christ, the Righteous. And His accomplishments (academic or otherwise) which qualify Him as our Representative are, above all, the all-sufficient atoning sacrifice which He brought "for our sins; and not for ours only but also for the sins of the whole world." (1 John 2:2)

The other Counsel, who advises us in the course which we are to pursue in presenting our prayers, is a Person who in character and ability is no whit behind the first Counsel. He is the Holy Spirit of God, whom the exalted Jesus has sent to be our Comforter, our Paraclete, One who constantly stands at our side. "And He who searches the hearts of men knows what is the mind of the Spirit, because the Spirit intercedes for the saints according to the will of God." (Romans 8:27 RSV)

Now, if, with these two mighty Advocates to assist us, we still fail to pray, then our first prayer ought to be: "Lord, teach us how to pray."

3.

Living the Prayer Life

"Lord, teach us to pray." Simple as the request is, it is basic to the Christian's prayer life, for to live the prayer life the Christian must learn how to pray.

"We have such a limited conception of prayer. We have said prayers, we have listened to prayers being said." We have cried out for help in trouble, we have even thanked God for sending deliverance. As routine pray-ers we are pretty good. We have learned the two words *give me* and, possibly, the other two, *thank you*. But if that is all we have learned, our prayer life is meager indeed.

The words *give me* as well as the words *thank you* are important and, like the words *Abba, Father,* very precious in prayer. We would not minimize their worth. But if we wish to live and fare well in the land of prayer, would it not be a mark of wisdom on our part to learn better the language that is spoken in that land?

Prayer is like a language that must be learned. At first we speak a broken language, but as we practice and learn to feel and to think the language, we come to speak it better and better. So it is with prayer. "Simple prayer, elementary prayer" (like elementary English) is, indeed, "within the grasp of the understanding of a little child; but the deeper lessons of prayer will test the ability of the greatest Christian prayer scholars and will give the best of us steady grist for our mills as long as we live" (C. E. Brown, *The Way of Prayer,* p. 17).

"Lord, teach us to pray." That's elemental. Prayer is something that has to be learned. And not only do we have to learn to pray; we must also learn how to pray.

Learning How to Pray

"Lord, teach us to pray." Coming from the disciples this was a strange request; for as Jews they had been taught to pray at regular intervals of the day. But observing Jesus in prayer, they realized that His praying was not "mere habit, no fulfilling of rules or regulations only." When some great need (mind you, *need* for the Son of Man) arose, He resorted to prayer for greater power — and received it — before choosing the twelve, after a mighty act of healing, after a hard day, when in sorrow over the death of Lazarus, before healing a lunatic. His prayer life was

55

rich; and the disciples were observing that prayer life in wonder and awe. "Lord, teach us to pray" was therefore a request for instruction in something besides routine prayer. The disciples wanted a lesson in prayer that is vital, powerful, effectual.

Jesus gave them the prayer of prayers; but He did not in that one brief moment give them a complete course in prayer. Not in so short a time can one master the noble art of prayer. At various other times Jesus, therefore, gave them further instruction in prayer; and they in turn, moved by the Holy Spirit, have for our sakes amplified and added to these instructions.

ACCORDING TO THE WILL OF GOD

It is essential to prayer that it conform to the divine will. We must pray according to God's will. Whatever our desire may be as we pray, our greatest desire must always be that God will in every given case, no matter what we pray for, always do what would be the wisest and the best, all things considered, for Him to do. This means that we desire, as we pray, that the answer to our prayer shall never violate the moral order which God has purposefully established in the universe. In its ultimate and sublimest this means that we say, "Thy will be done."

But how can we always know if what we ask is in accordance with God's will? We can't — not always.

However, with proper discipline we can learn to pray more and more according to God's will. God has in many instances revealed His will to us, and

56

if we but take the time and the trouble to search it out, we shall know what His will is. According to it we pray.

In His Word God has revealed what is His will with regard to the world and to us; and whatever we now ask for within the limits of that revealed will is according to His will. "God will have all men to be saved and to come unto the knowledge of the truth" (1 Timothy 2:4). What a large area is here opened up for us to pray according to God's will! "This is the will of God, even your sanctification" (1 Thessalonians 4:3). Let us carefully study this area of prayer before we begin to complain that we do not know how to pray according to God's will. "He which hath begun a good work in you will perform it until the day of Jesus Christ" (Philippians 1:6). No, I need not forget myself or my eternal welfare when I pray according to God's will. "Father," so prayed Jesus, our Savior, "I will that they also whom Thou hast given Me be with Me where I am, that they may behold My glory" (John 17:24). Does the stipulation that we pray according to God's will restrict or limit us in our prayer? No. The scope of our prayer is still eternal.

That's why God wants us to pray according to His will. His eternal purpose for our welfare must be accomplished. We would not want it otherwise. We want the desire that the eternal purpose and will of God be realized to overshadow all our other desires. So did Jesus pray in Gethsemane. "Father, if Thou be willing, remove this cup from Me. Nevertheless not My will, but Thine, be done" (Luke 22:42). The cup was not removed, though Jesus prayed for its removal if it could be removed without interrupting God's eternal plan of salvation. Overshadowing the prayer for the removal of the cup was the prayer that God's will be carried through; and this prayer was abundantly answered — as we, God be praised, can testify. If we learn to place God's will above our desires, if we learn to let God's will overshadow our desires, if we learn to yield our desires to the will of God, if we learn to harmonize our will with His, we know that our prayers will be answered. "This is the confidence that we have in Him, that if we ask anything according to His will, He heareth us." (1 John 5:14)

As we pray according to the will of God, we agree also that the answer to prayer shall do no injury to the one who prays. If it would, the prayer would be too ambitious, like the prayer of a boy who asks his father for a razor. He might injure himself. As years pass, the father may well give him a razor; but at the moment he will tell his boy, "No." We are reminded of the ambitious prayer of the mother of Zebedee's children. Inspired, no doubt, by James and John themselves, she came to Jesus with the request, "Grant that these my two sons may sit, the one on Thy right hand and the other on the left, in Thy kingdom." Jesus told her and them, "Ye know not what ye ask" (Matthew 20:20-22). Again, the prayer would be too shortsighted, like the prayer of a child who asks its mother not to be sent to school. As the years pass, the mother will acquiesce; but for the time being the child needs to go to school. We are reminded of St. Paul praying, not once or twice, but three times, for the removal of the thorn that was tormenting him. The thorn was not removed. Years later, when he was glorying in his infirmities (2 Corinthians 12:5), he was still marveling at the answer which he had received from the Lord: "My grace is sufficient for thee, for My strength is made perfect in weakness." St. Paul appreciated the lesson which the Lord had taught him. He said, "Most gladly therefore will I rather glory in my infirmities, that the power of Christ may rest upon me" (2 Corinthians 12:9). It is a lesson that is not altogether too easy to learn, that pain, suffering, bereavement, sorrow, toil are a part of the moral discipline not only of the human race in general but also of the Christian in particular, and that it is not God's will that by prayer we should evade them entirely. "We must through much tribulation enter into the kingdom of God." (Acts 14:22)

As we pray according to the will of God, we agree also that the answer to our prayer must not in any case injure anyone else unjustly. No Christian would knowingly pray such a prayer. And if he inadvertently would fall into the error of so doing, Jesus would answer him, as He answered the ambitious sons of thunder, when they, irked by the impertinence of the Samaritans, asked Him, "Lord, wilt Thou that we command fire to come down from heaven and consume them, even as Elias did?" Sharply did He rebuke them: "Ye know not what manner of spirit ye are of. For the Son of Man is not come to destroy men's lives, but to save them." (Luke 9:54-56)

And yet for all that, though God wants us to pray according to His will, though He has in His Word revealed all that we need to know concerning His will, and though "the Spirit also helpeth our infirmities," we still do not always know "what we should pray for as we ought" (Romans 8:26). And because we do not know and whenever we do not know, we pray that God would grant our request if it be His will.

One thing more needs to be said in this connection. Prayer dare not be dictation. We may plead. We may promise. We may even bargain. But never ought we to deliver an ultimatum. That principle is axiomatic. Nor ought we ever dictate to God the precise manner in which our prayer shall be answered, for to do so would be to question the wisdom of God. Under the pressure of anxiety Christians may sometimes come dangerously close to doing just that, though they really do not mean to. The Lord will not condemn them for it, as little as He condemned His mother when she interceded for the Cana household; for to outline the manner is not the same as to deliver an ultimatum. Doubtless He will correct them, as He corrected her; but doubtless, too, no lasting harm will come from this kind of prayer provided we are ready to leave the details to the wisdom of God.

In his book *The Way of Prayer* (pp. 131 f.) C. E. Brown tells us: "A story comes from the early ages of the church. The saintly Monica was the mother of a brilliant but wild and godless youth, Augustine.

Often and long did she pray for his salvation. At last there came a fateful night. Somehow she learned that on that night her poor, scapegrace son had planned to board a ship and run away from home to Italy. The very thought of her poor, wild, passionate son throwing himself into the maelstrom of vice and unbelief whirling throughout imperial Italy simply broke her heart insomuch that she spent the whole night praying that God might save her son and restrain him from going to Italy. And that night while she was in prayer, the stubborn youth boarded the ship and sailed away. Most certainly this seems like the complete denial of a most sincere and godly request. Yet it was not so in God's sight, for the Lord knew that in Milan, Italy, was a minister of God, Ambrose, saint and preacher of the Gospel, who, like Augustine, was a brilliant and gifted man and probably the only man in all the world who could influence Augustine and turn his heart to God. All unknown to Augustine and to his saintly mother, God turned the steps of the brilliant young pagan toward Italy and toward Milan, where he met Saint Ambrose and was soundly converted to Christianity, later becoming the most distinguished teacher of the Christian Church for the next one thousand years. Undoubtedly, Monica's prayers were answered, but not exactly in the way in which she had specified and expected." I doubt very much whether in her anxiety for the spiritual welfare of her wayward son she meant to dictate to God. Methinks she prayed according to the will of God, and her prayers were answered in a way that would please a Christian mother's heart.

61

One of the greatest lessons in prayer which Jesus taught His disciples He reserved for the crisis hour before His betrayal and His death. Clearly He enunciated and repeated the principal as He bade them farewell. "Whatsoever ye shall ask in My name, that will I do, that the Father may be glorified in the Son. If ye shall ask anything in My name, I will do it" (John 14:13, 14). "Ye have not chosen Me, but I have chosen you and ordained you that ye should go and bring forth fruit and that your fruit should remain, that whatsoever ye shall ask of the Father in My name, He may give it you" (John 15:16). "And in that day ye shall ask Me nothing. Verily, verily, I say unto you, Whatsoever ye shall ask the Father in My name, He will give it you. Hitherto have ye asked nothing in My name; ask, and ye shall receive that your joy may be full" (John 16:23, 24). "At that day ye shall ask in My name; and I say not unto you that I will pray the Father for you, for the Father Himself loveth you because ye have loved Me and have believed that I came out from God" (John 16: 26, 27). From these directives it is very evident that the disciples not only were given the privilege but were instructed to direct their petitions to God in the name of Jesus Christ.

What does this phrase mean? If one may judge by the way some people use the phrase, praying in Jesus Christ's name means to them no more than simply using the formula "This we ask in Jesus' name," or some equivalent expression. But, as proper as such a formula is, praying in Jesus' name means more than just to use that formula. In his *Christian Prayer* (pp. 15 f.) in answer to the question, "What does this phrase mean?" William Arndt says, "Somebody might think that what is enjoined thereby is that you have to mention the name of Jesus in your prayer and that such mention is the magic key which opens the treasure-house of God to the petitioners and permits them to take what they please. That such an opinion would be wrong we see at once from the model prayer which Jesus has taught us. The name of Jesus does not occur in it, which is quite convincing proof that a prayer, to be proper and acceptable, does not necessarily have to contain the name of Jesus. Certainly we like to mention the name of our blessed Savior when we speak to God, and we often conclude our petitions by saying, 'This we ask in the name of Jesus.' Every Christian will have to admit that such phraseology is beautiful and to be commended. But what needs to be said here is that these words are not essential and that a prayer may be uttered in the name of Jesus without employment of that particular phrase. While we gladly join this phrase to our prayer to remind ourselves that our petitions must be spoken in the name of our heavenly Lord, the question presents itself as one ponders the subject a little more whether merely the insertion of the words 'This we ask in the name of Jesus' actually in every case makes the prayer one that is truly spoken in the name of our divine Master — a question which, we must sadly admit, is to be answered in the negative."

What, then, does it mean to pray in the name of Jesus, or to pray in the name of Christ? It means to pray "with faith in Him as our Redeemer." It means that when we pray, and as we pray, and for what we pray, we rely for our acceptance and for an answer on the redemption that Jesus has wrought for us. Here is the situation: We are sinners, crimson sinners, unworthy sinners. "We are worthy of none of the things for which we pray, neither have we deserved them." How can we expect an audience, let alone an answer? Jesus reaches out His hand and says, "I am the Way, the Truth, and the Life; no man cometh unto the Father but by Me" (John 14:6). We clasp that hand, enter boldly "into the holiest by the blood of Jesus" (Hebrews 10:19), and plead, "For His sake, good Lord, for His sake." — It takes a humble person to pray in the name of Jesus.

To pray in the name of Jesus also contains the promise that if our prayer be granted we intend the answer to redound to His glory. It stands to reason that what we get in the name of Jesus is to be used in His service and in the promotion of His business and purpose. This does not limit our prayers; it gives them proper direction. It keeps our prayers from being self-centered in purpose. It does happen, for instance, that people when praying for health add "in the name of Jesus" with the idea that when health is restored they can use their lives for selfish pleasure more satisfactorily than while in a state of illness. No one praying in such an attitude can be said to be praying in Jesus' name, though he may be using the formula. What he seeks he is not seeking for the glory of God. He asks for the satisfaction of his own selfish desire, and that attitude blemishes his prayer.

64

"Whatsoever ye do, do all to the glory of God" (1 Corinthians 10:31) is a guiding principle also in prayer. It is because this guiding principle is so often lost sight of that the prayers of many receive as little divine attention as they do; for these are the prayers which the apostle James referred to when he wrote: "Ye ask and receive not, because ye ask amiss, that ye may consume it upon your lusts." (James 4:3)

To pray in the name of Jesus is a distinct privilege, for it opens the way to the Father and assures success to our prayer venture. The privilege, however, is not without its corresponding stewardship responsibility: that we consecrate ourselves and the answer to our prayer to Jesus and His cause. To pray in the name of Jesus a person must be consecrated.

IN THE POWER OF THE SPIRIT

To pray in the name of Jesus means at the same time to pray in the power of the Spirit. The one truth involves the other. When Jesus left His disciples, He promised to send the Spirit to take His place. While Jesus, in whose name we pray, is our representative in heaven, assuring acceptance of our prayers, the Holy Spirit, in whose power we pray, is His representative in our hearts, teaching us how to pray. These two facts are closely linked together in our prayer life.

Without the Holy Spirit's assistance our prayers would be woefully deficient, for we are so hesitant, so infirm, so given to wavering. We need the power of the Spirit to stabilize our prayers and to give them proper expression. "The Spirit also helpeth our infirmities," writes St. Paul, whose words are so very much to the point — "the Spirit also helpeth our infirmities; for we know not what we should pray for [RSV: how to pray] as we ought; but the Spirit Itself maketh intercession for us with groanings which cannot be uttered." (Romans 8:26)

What the indwelling Spirit teaches about prayer is not new. For He teaches us to pray as Jesus prayed and as Jesus taught His disciples to pray — as children, trustful and confident. When Jesus taught His disciples to pray, He taught them to say, "Our Father." Later when He prayed His greatest prayer, He prayed thus: "Abba, Father." That prayer was accompanied by the entire surrender and sacrifice of His life and His love. In the same spirit the Holy Spirit teaches us to pray. "Ye have received the Spirit of adoption, whereby we cry, Abba, Father," writes St. Paul to the Romans (8:15); and to the Galatians (4:6) he writes, "God hath sent the Spirit of His Son into your hearts, crying, Abba, Father."

It is in prayer that we learn more fully to appreciate the promise of the Savior: "I will pray the Father, and He shall give you another Comforter, that He may abide with you forever, even the Spirit of truth, whom the world cannot receive, because it seeth Him not neither knoweth Him; but ye know Him, for He dwelleth with you and shall be in you" (John 14:16, 17). In prayer this promise finds its practical worth, for in our prayer there is a wonderful, a complete blending of co-operation between the Spirit and us. In the passage just quoted from Romans we read, "We cry, Abba, Father." In the passage just quoted from Galatians we read, "He cries, Abba, Father." Giving us the opportunity to pray in the power of the Spirit, God has done His utmost to make prayer foolproof for us; for if the Holy Spirit co-operates in our prayers even to the extent that He inspires them, guides them, and stabilizes them, we have the assurance that, as we pray in His power, we need have no misgivings as to whether we are praying according to the will of God; for "He that searcheth the hearts knoweth what is the mind of the Spirit, because He maketh intercession for the saints according to the will of God" (Romans 8:27). God has indeed done His utmost to make prayer foolproof for us.

Another thing to keep in mind is this: As we pray in the power of the indwelling Spirit, we are reminded of God's desire for human fellowship, and that reminder makes prayer very real, almost dreadfully, yet reassuringly real. Through His Holy Spirit God Himself is present; He is here, listening to us as we pray — here — not afar off — but here. How easy it is to pray to Him, to talk with Him, even to whisper to Him — in the power of the Spirit.

IN FAITH

If we pray in the power of the Spirit, we shall pray in faith; and in faith we must pray. "Have faith in God," says Jesus, "for verily I say unto you, that whosoever shall say unto this mountain, Be thou removed, and be thou cast into the sea, and shall not doubt in his heart but shall believe that those things which he saith shall come to pass, he shall have whatsoever he saith. Therefore I say unto you, What things soever ye desire, when ye pray, believe that ye receive them, and ye shall have them." (Mark 11:22-24)

We do not believe those words! We do not half believe them! We show by our very hesitancy that we do not. If we believed them, we would dare to ask for greater things — and receive them; for doesn't the Savior say, "All things whatsoever ye shall ask in prayer, believing, ye shall receive"? (Matthew 21:22). The sad truth is that we do not really believe in the power of prayer. We do not dare believe, because we fear that God will not or cannot respond to our prayer. — An awful indictment! to our shame! No wonder we are so often disappointed in prayer! "Let him ask in faith," writes St. James (1:6-8), "nothing wavering. For he that wavereth is like a wave of the sea driven with the wind and tossed. For let not that man think that he shall receive anything of the Lord. A double-minded man [a double-souled man, now trusting, now distrusting] is unstable in all his ways."

We see the Savior coming down from the Mount of Transfiguration to His frustrated disciples, and we hear Him saying, "O faithless and perverse generation, how long shall I be with you and suffer you?" (Luke 9:41), and shamefacedly we drop our heads and pray, "Lord, we believe; help Thou our unbelief. We do not believe in the power of prayer. We don't! We don't! — Oh, but we do! We do! We want to! Lord, we believe; help Thou our unbelief!" (Cf. Mark 9:24). And the Lord is ready to help us believe. To

68

strengthen our faith He promises us: "Ask, and it shall be given you; seek, and ye shall find; knock, and it shall be opened unto you; for everyone that asketh receiveth and he that seeketh findeth; and to him that knocketh it shall be opened" (Matthew 7:7, 8). This promise must certainly inspire us to greater confidence.

It is so easy to prevail with God. A little faith, a very little faith, a mustard-seed faith, almost no faith at all will go far in prevailing with the wonderful God who fashioned this unthinkable, immeasurable universe out of nothing and made man, with his dreams and aspirations and achievements, out of a little common dust — frail man. A hesitating touch on the hem of Christ's garment by one too shy and too frightened to speak to Him at all, can work wonders! "Lord, we believe; help Thou our unbelief!" We may be astonished at His promise; we may be staggered by it; but let us be humbly grateful for it and believe; for faith in God's willingness and ability to hear and answer must accompany our every prayer. "I will therefore that men pray everywhere, lifting up holy hands, without wrath and doubting" (1 Timothy 2:8). And certainly after Calvary God has a right to be trusted, to be believed that He means what He says; for in Christ all His promises are yea and in Him Amen.

IN SINCERITY

A prayer of faith must and will at the same time be a prayer of sincerity. This means not only that we should not pray for things which we really do not want but also that we pray with an honesty of heart and spirit that God expects of His children.

Be honest with God. Do not lie. Do not play the hypocrite. Do not try to deceive God. You can't fool the All-wise. "Who shall ascend into the hill of the Lord? Or who shall stand in His holy place? He that hath clean hands and a pure heart; who hath not lifted up his soul unto vanity [to what is false] nor sworn deceitfully. He shall receive the blessing from the Lord and righteousness from the God of his salvation." (Psalm 24:3-5)

We are once again confronted with a paradox. "Clean hands and a pure heart" are demanded. We are sinners, unclean every whit, and well might we ask: "Who can bring a clean thing out of an unclean" (Job 14:4) to enable us to approach the Lord with clean hands and a pure heart? But the unclean has been sprinkled (cp. Hebrews 9:13). "The blood of Jesus Christ, His Son, cleanseth us from all sin" (1 John 1:7). We may approach. We may stand in His holy place; only let us be sincere. Referring to the beneficial effect of the Old Testament sacrifices, the apostle writes in his letter to the Hebrews: "How much more shall the blood of Christ, who through the eternal spirit offered Himself without spot to God, purge your conscience from dead works to serve the living God?" (Hebrews 9:14.) Our intention must conform to that purpose as we approach God in prayer. "I will therefore," writes St. Paul, "that men pray everywhere, lifting up holy hands, without wrath or doubting." (1 Timothy 2:8)

Anyone who refuses to give up his wrath, his pride, his greed, his intemperance, his sensuality, certainly would do better not to pray, for his prayer would be quite insincere and would serve only to harden him in his wickedness. Just before the climax of his drama *Hamlet* Shakespeare has the miserable wretch of a king soliloquize:

O, my offence is rank, it smells to heaven;
It hath the primal oldest curse upon 't,
A brother's murder. Pray can I not,
Though inclination be as sharp as will:
My stronger guilt defeats my strong intent;
And, like a man to double business bound,
I stand in pause where I shall first begin,
And both neglect. . . .
. . . But, O, what form of prayer
Can serve my turn? 'Forgive me my foul murder'?
That cannot be; since I am still possess'd
Of those effects for which I did the murder,
My crown, mine own ambition and my queen.
May one be pardon'd and retain the offence?

(Act III, Scene 3)

How can a person sincerely pray for the forgiveness of sins when he secretly purposes to pursue the same evil way he has trod so long? How can he sincerely pray not to be tempted when he already secretly relishes the thought of another temptation? How can he sincerely pray to be saved from the power of the evil one when he has no intention of serving the Holy One with an honest heart? How can he sincerely pray "Hallowed be Thy name" when he will not let God's name be hallowed in his heart and life? No sin is so great that it should ever hinder prayer (let it be but sincerely repented of), but no sin is so small as not to be able to turn prayer itself into sin if the heart that means to pray does not sincerely intend to resist the sin. "If I regard iniquity in my heart, the Lord will not hear me" (Psalm 66:18). Yet if a man sins seven times, nay, seventy times seven, and as often sincerely turns to God and asks for power and strength to overcome his sins, God will hear and answer his prayer.

WITH UNDERSTANDING

When we pray it is important that we know what we are praying and what we are praying for. We must pray with the understanding (the mind) also. This important rule St. Paul sets forth in his first letter to the Corinthians (14:15): "I will pray with the spirit, and I will pray with the understanding also." Some of the Christians under Paul's pastorate thought that so-called ecstatic prayer (prayer with the spirit) was the very acme of prayer, even though it were but a babbling of tongues. St. Paul told them that to pray in an ecstatic utterance of unknown language would not edify or help one who did not understand that language. St. Paul added that he would rather speak five words with his understanding than ten thousand words in an unknown tongue. Our intellect, too, must be placed into the service of faith; and prayer, which is an exercise of faith, must be an exercise of the understanding also. Prayer is not merely a matter of feeling and emotion, but of the intellect, the understanding, as well. If we wish to pray sincerely, confidently, and earnestly, if we wish to have our prayer be more than a mere jumble of words and empty

72

phrases, we must pray intelligently and thoughtfully — "with the understanding also."

To pray with the understanding calls for concentration. This is one of the most toilsome and tiring things that we human beings have to do, and sometimes we are too lazy even to follow vicariously a train of prayer thoughts carefully worked out by another, to say nothing of our readiness to concentrate on prayer objects of our own thinking. Yet, if we do not keep our prayer steadfastly in mind or if we allow some other thought to usurp the place of the prayer which we are urging before God, even the Lord's Prayer becomes a vain repetition. The wretched king in *Hamlet* spoke true when he said:

> *My words fly up, my thoughts remain below:*
> *Words without thoughts never to heaven go.*
> *(Act III, Scene 3)*

To enable us to pray with the understanding we must particularize our prayers. The vague and the general will not do. There must be some particular thing to which the understanding can attach itself; otherwise, as we lose ourselves in large generalities, our prayers will die of vagueness. To say that too often we thank God "for all the blessings of life" may sound like a contradiction of truth. But the fact is that this concept is far too large for the average mind. Count your blessings.

> *Count your many blessings,*
> *Name them one by one,*
> *Count your many blessings,*
> *See what God has done.*

Break down the concept into its component parts, otherwise it is too indefinite and remains a vague blur, and the pray-er does not really know what he is thanking God for.

The psalmist does indeed encourage us, "Bless the Lord, O my soul, and forget not all His benefits" (Psalm 103:2), but he nicely breaks that concept down into its component parts and goes into detail. He particularizes: "Who forgiveth all thine iniquities, who healeth all thy diseases, who redeemeth thy life from destruction, who crowneth thee with loving-kindness and tender mercies, who satisfieth thy mouth with good things, so that thy youth is renewed like the eagle's" (Psalm 103:3-5). Similarly St. Paul instructs us "I exhort, therefore, that, first of all, supplications, prayers, intercessions, and giving of thanks be made for all men" — a large concept that — which he breaks down into its component parts by continuing, "for kings and for all that are in authority" (1 Timothy 2:1, 2). When we in compliance with this instruction pray "for all that are in authority" we shall further aid our understanding by praying specifically for the President, the Governor, and the senators and representatives, that God may give them sane judgment and keep them from foolish and harmful vagaries. Our prayers would be more vital and vibrant if we followed the example of our children, who pray God to bless mamma and papa and sister and brother, and concentrate on particular needs, particular desires, and particular purposes.

To enable us to pray with understanding we shall do well to keep our own personal prayers simple and

74

to simplify some of our formal prayers. Far be it from me to disparage formal prayers. They have their place and serve their purpose. Their thought plane is often lofty and their phraseology majestic. But in their strength lies their weakness. Majestically their thoughts march through the mind without prevailing upon the mind to fall into step. And before the mind has a chance to sink into them and to use them in thoughtful prayer, they are gone. For private prayer they may be ideal; for then we can lingeringly brood over the thoughts and slowly think them through and crumble them into their component details; but to repeat them, or to listen to them being spoken, gives the inexpert little chance to participate.

To enable us to pray with understanding we must pray slower than we sometimes do, especially when we pray as a group. Too often we seem to be in too great a hurry. In some instances the Lord's Prayer has been prayed so rapidly that I have had to fall out because both my lips and my mind were too slow to keep up with the tempo and still keep the direction of the prayer. And many others must have felt just like that. That is mechanical prayer, mere patter. And does not the word "patter" come from the Pater Nosters, the Lord's Prayers, which in the Latin were often repeated in a very rapid and mechanical way? If the Lord takes time to listen, we ought to take time to pray "with the understanding also."

To enable us to pray with understanding, particularly when praying as a group, we ought to use long prayers rather sparingly. Again let it be said that long prayers have their place and serve their purpose, but

75

the great mass of ordinary worshipers just cannot long follow in the wake of long prayers. One by one they fall out and are left behind. They may still be listening but no longer praying. Many of our great prayers — the Lord's Prayer, the General Confession, many of the collects — how brief they are, yet how heaped-up and how satisfying! If or when longer prayers are called for, we shall do well to break them up, following the example of the litanies, which are longer prayers broken up into shorter sections. "Keep thy foot when thou goest to the house of God, and be more ready to hear than to give the sacrifice of fools; for they consider not that they do evil" (Ecclesiastes 5:1). These words have a familiar ring because we have frequently heard them. But let us this once continue, "Be not rash with thy mouth, and let not thine heart be hasty to utter anything before God; for God is in heaven and thou upon earth; therefore let thy words be few." (Ecclesiastes 5:2)

If we exercise the proper care, it will not be too difficult to pray "with the understanding also."

WITH PERSISTENCE

We pray according to the will of God, in the name of Jesus Christ, in the power of the Holy Spirit, in faith, in sincerity, and with the understanding also. But nothing happens; we have no tangible evidence that our prayers are heard or answered. Do we quit? Do we cease just because we have come to the point where prayer becomes toil? No. The Savior wants us to be persistent in our prayer.

In several of His parables the Savior dwelt on this very feature of persistency in prayer and earnestly urged that it be cultivated. There is the parable of a certain man who at midnight aroused his friend and pestered him for bread, because he had received hungry company and had nothing to eat in the house. He got his bread. "And I say unto you," said Jesus, "Ask, and it shall be given you; seek, and ye shall find; knock, and it shall be opened unto you." (Luke 11:5-9)

The classic example of persistency in prayer, however, we have in the parable of the Importunate Widow. Here is the way we have it told in the Revised Standard Version: "And Jesus told them a parable, to the effect that they ought always to pray and not lose heart. He said, 'In a certain city there was a judge who neither feared God nor regarded man; and there was a widow in that city who kept coming to him and saying, "Vindicate me against my adversary." For a while he refused; but afterward he said to himself, "Though I neither fear God nor regard man, yet because this widow bothers me, I will vindicate her, or she will wear me out by her continual coming." ' And the Lord said, 'Hear what the unrighteous judge says. And will not God vindicate His elect, who cry to Him day and night? Will He delay long over them? I tell you, He will vindicate them speedily'" (Luke 18:1-8). This parable urges persistence in prayer by contrasting a certain judge with God. First, the judge did not fear God, nor did he regard man. He was selfish, self-centered, ruthless, and unjust. God, on the other hand, is deeply concerned about man and absolutely righteous. He will do justice by all who come to Him. That is the first contrast. There is another contrast. In order to persuade the unjust judge, annoying, even humiliating persistence (importunity) was necessary. He was selfish and self-centered, but because the widow went to him again and again, he, to get rid of her lest she wear him out by her continual coming, yielded to her request. Importunity, however, is never necessary to persuade God — persistence, yes, but never importunity. God will vindicate His petitioners speedily. God is so full of compassion, so full of might, so full of infinite and strict integrity and justice that the plea of the weakest, the feeblest, the frailest soul brings an answer. He is a God ready to hear and to answer, ready to place His omnipotence at the disposal of the saint who prays to Him. Therefore men "ought always to pray and not to lose heart." St. Paul says, "Be constant in prayer" (Romans 12:12, RSV). It is here that we would like to apply also his directive, "Pray without ceasing" (1 Thessalonians 5:17). This simply means, "Don't be discouraged. Keep on praying."

WITH HUMILITY

Persistency in prayer, however, does not give us the license to become impertinent. We must remain reverent and humble.

In the midst of the stress and the strain of life great souls have sometimes given way to impertinence. Jeremiah, contemplating the miseries of Judah, spoke words wholly unbecoming the prophet: "Ah,

78

Lord God, surely Thou hast greatly deceived this people and Jerusalem, saying, Ye shall have peace; whereas the sword reacheth unto the soul!" (Jeremiah 4:10)

God deserves our reverence also, and especially, in prayer. It was reverence in the heart of Moses to which the Lord appealed when He appeared to him in the burning bush; for when the Lord revealed Himself as the God of Amram, the God of Abraham, the God of Isaac, and the God of Jacob, "Moses hid his face; for he was afraid to look upon God" (Exodus 3:1-6). Our modern age has been taught "not to fear God, and as a result we have a generation which, although it is remarkably free from that fear, seems to suffer from nearly every other kind of fear men have ever known" (Brown, p. 22). Teach men to come to God with due reverence, and many of their other fears will soon be dispelled. As "the fear of the Lord is the beginning of wisdom" (Psalm 111:10), so the fear of the Lord, the attitude of love mingled with awe, fear moderated by the trust which we have in the Lord's goodness and love, in other words, reverence, is essential to Christian prayer.

At the burning bush Moses was instructed to remove his shoes. This is still the customary sign of humility in the Orient when a suppliant enters a temple or a place of worship. God seeks humility in the hearts of His petitioners. "Thus saith the High and Lofty One that inhabiteth eternity, whose name is Holy; I dwell in the high and holy place, with him also that is of a contrite and humble spirit, to revive the spirit of the humble and to revive the heart of the

79

contrite ones" (Isaiah 57:15). We must shed the pride of the Pharisee, who in prayer thanked God that he was not like other men; we must shun the selfish ambition of the sons of Zebedee, who in prayer requested that Jesus give them a prominent position above others; and with a humble heart approach the Lord and say, "God, be merciful to me, a sinner."

And if we come humbly, we may come very simply. We shall not need to study philosophy or systematic theology. We shall not need to speculate on how far it is to the eternal throne or whether the Lord is able to hear us. Though the sea of glass spoken of in Revelation (4:6) is wider than light could cross in a hundred years, for the eyes of faith the throne of God stands in our prayer closets, the garments of God sweep across the floors of our humble dwellings, and even though we kneel in the loam of the freshly turned furrow, we can reach forth the hand of faith and touch the wounds of the Nazarene, who gave Himself for us. We do not have to guess about this. We have God's own words as our assurance. He says: "To this man will I look, even to him that is poor and of a contrite spirit and trembleth at My Word." (Isaiah 66:2; cf. Psalm 34:18; 51:17)

IN THE SPIRIT OF SUBMISSIVENESS

We come now to the acid test of humble prayer: the spirit of submissiveness.

To pray submissively is not the same as to accept the will of God with a silent acquiescence. Jesus did not pray thus; yet He left us the classic example of a submissive prayer. He suggested, He pleaded, He battled, He wrestled, He agonized, He sweat blood, the while He was ready to submit Himself to the Father's will. God does want us to storm His heart and is pleased at times, upon being persuaded, to yield His will to ours. However, if in His love and wisdom He must refuse our request, we must anticipate His response and say, "Nevertheless not my will, but Thine, be done."

Have you ever given the command of God to Abraham personal thought? "Take now thy son . . . whom thou lovest . . . and offer him" (Genesis 22:2). The command can come with startling suddenness. I know a father, the same man who through his fervent prayer had previously wrested the wife of his youth from the claws of death, who had a son of ten years — a good little boy. The little son had what one doctor has called "one of the most malignant afflictions that can visit a human being." In a desperate attempt to relieve the affliction and to save the boy's life an operation was attempted. The little boy never regained consciousness. The father prayed, the mother prayed — the boy died. God did not yield His will to the will of the suppliants. Why not? I do not know. Certainly the father prayed hard, for on that bed there lay unconscious the little jewel of his heart. His prayer was sincere and perhaps more fervent than any prayer he ever prayed. On Maundy Thursday evening it was that the father, who all the while had been ready to submit, said, "Thy will be done. Spare the child further anguish"; and on the next day at noon,

81

on the stroke of twelve, in the darkness of Good Friday the angels carried the soul of the little child into the realms of heavenly light. The father submitted — at first, it may be, because he had to, but gradually over the years, as the grief mellowed and hallowed, because his will had yielded to God's will. He learned from experience how hard it can be to pray, "Thy will be done" — not only in submission, but also in faith and love. To submit to God's will, this is comparatively less difficult; but to submit — and to keep on loving and trusting — is an art best learned in the school of experience. "Nevertheless not my will, but Thine, be done."

WITH A READINESS TO CO-OPERATE WITH GOD

In prayer, as in everything else, it is important to keep the proper balance. Prayer has many facets, and if we want to live a balanced prayer life, we must not let our imagination concentrate on one facet only.

For the purpose which we have in mind, prayer may be roughly divided into two kinds: mystic prayer and prophetic prayer. Mystic prayer stresses the passive attitude of self-abandonment and self-abasement, whereas prophetic prayer stresses the active, the accomplishment of the thing prayed for. Neither should be misapplied, neither should be overemphasized at the expense of the other, and between the two we should keep a proper balance.

Proponents of mystic prayer frequently take the extreme view that prayer is a kind of spiritual therapy only and that the sole object of prayer is to leave the soul completely passive and submissive under the rolling waves of the ocean of life. They have learned, they say, that prayer may, after all, be a very simple exercise. Time was, they will admit, when they informed God of their needs and their desires and pleaded with Him to intervene in their behalf; but so perfectly have they now disciplined their souls that their prayers have become very short. "Lord, You know better than I what is good for me. Do as You please, and I shall be satisfied." But he who supposes that the answer to prayer consists only in a change in oneself, to the end that his own will be finally brought into harmony with God's will, has not yet understood the full function of prayer. God has, after all, commanded us to pray and has promised to hear us. His ordinance of prayer guarantees and assures an answer to prayer also in a prophetic way. By inviting us to pray He has hung out for us the latchstring to His omnipotence.

But the proponents of prophetic prayer should not take the view that prayer, because of its prophetic action, is some kind of magic which short-circuits all thought, all toil, and all discipline of life. "Prayer," says Arndt, "must not be considered a sort of magic by means of which we obtain what we desire or a substitute for the faithful use of our bodily and mental faculties in meeting our problems" (p. 47). "It will not do for us," writes Gossip "to roll the burden upon God, and then lounge back at our ease, expecting Him to put what others gained by long and hard-breathing endeavor into our soft unroughened hands that show no trace of honest toil." (P. 25)

83

To keep a proper balance between these two, mystic prayer and prophetic prayer, we must pray with a spirit of ready co-operation.

Three kings, marching against an invader, stood on the brink of disaster, because in the vast desert somewhere south of the Dead Sea they had failed to find water for their armies at the place they had expected to find it. It was a forbidding country with temperatures ranging up to 130 degrees in the shade. Pitilessly the sun beat down upon man and beast. In their helpless condition the kings, Jehoram of Israel, Jehoshaphat of Judah, and the king of Edom, turned to God by inquiring of His propet Elisha, the son of Shaphat. Doubtless everyone would have expected God to send showers of rain. But the prophet Elisha commanded them to dig ditches, which on the morrow at the time of the meat offering were filled with water (2 Kings 3:6-20). This incident in the Old Testament teaches much concerning prayer. Though I must firmly believe and do firmly believe that God is able to answer my prayers by either applying or suspending natural laws — for He Himself is not bound nor limited by the laws which He Himself has created — yet there is no doubt in my mind that God prefers to operate through natural laws wherever possible and that He therefore expects us, in answer to our own prayers, to observe the natural physical laws and to help ourselves as much as possible.

When we pray for help, we cannot always expect God to do all the work. We would be like children who ask for roller skates when they could easily forego treats and from their allowance save up for them, who ask God to make them good boys and girls but are rather slow to co-operate in the endeavor, who ask God to bless mother but do not think at all of helping her or being kind to her. We would want God to do all the work and to be our handyman to do all our difficult and distasteful tasks for us.

Suppose I should sit down to my table and pray, "Lord, be pleased to give me beef." Were I a farmer, He would inform me that I might pretty well raise my own beef; and were I a laborer, He would tell me that the butcher would be happy to talk the problem over with me. Or suppose I should stand by a crab-apple tree and pray, "Lord, I have a taste for pears. Make pears grow on this tree." His answer might well be, "Certainly, if you will graft it." If I neglected to follow His advice, I would get no pears from that tree. Or suppose I were sick. If relief lay in the realm of the natural and I prayed and did nothing more, I would find no relief until I came to my senses and consulted a skillful physician. In our extremities God does adopt special and extraordinary means to help us in answer to our prayers, as when He sent an angel to deliver the apostle Peter from prison; but if Peter had had a passkey in his pocket and had had the power to use it but had failed to use it, we would not have expected the angel to appear on the scene.

Some lay down the proposition that God will not do anything for us that we can do for ourselves. This statement seems to be too sweeping. St. Paul tells us that we are "workers together with God." "If we work together with God, it seems only reasonable to conclude that God will work together with us — also in the realm of prayer. We have a full right to expect of God that He will help us in our work. [God helped me in this work, but He certainly also made me work.] The work which we do to help ourselves, we do in His strength and with His aid, and we fully realize that we could not otherwise do it. Nevertheless we must not abuse this principle and privilege and expect God to do the work which we can full well do ourselves and which is primarily our duty and responsibility" (cf. Brown, p. 133). Prayer must never degenerate into an argument for laziness. If a thing is accessible to a person through natural means, God expects him to exert his own energies, even after he has prayed for it, in order to obtain it.

Ideally, a Christian works as if he has to do it all and prays as if he can't do a thing.

FOLLOWING PATTERN OF FORMAL PRAYERS

To learn the art of prayer we shall do well to study the prayers of others which have stood the test of time and answer to the needs of countless numbers of people. These we call formal prayers. The term refers to all prayers which are not original and spontaneous at the time of praying, and particularly does it refer to written prayers.

Some think formal prayers stereotyped. Some may be; but certainly not all can be summarily put into that class. That many of the best formal prayers follow a definite pattern does not make them stereotyped but only proves that they contain the recognized essentials of prayer.

Some are prejudiced against formal prayers because, they say, they are just that, formal — too formal. Not expressing their personal desires, they become for such people only a vain repetition of words. This need not be the fault of the prayers. It may be the fault of the one using the prayers. And if it is the fault of the pray-er, then it may be equally true that his extemporaneous prayers may at times also be "just saying words," and "poorly chosen words at that." (Garrett, p. 18)

By studying and by using formal prayers, both Biblical and extra-Biblical, we get into the stream of Christian tradition. We avail ourselves of the help of experts in the field of prayer. They got where we want to get to, and their prayers helped them to get there. We would be foolish not to study them and use them.

Take the pearl of all formal prayers, the Lord's Prayer. Analyzing it, as the Lord taught it in His Sermon on the Mount, we clearly discern the outline, which many formal prayers have adopted:

The address: "Our Father";

The descriptive clause: "Which art in heaven";

The petition: "Hallowed be Thy name. Thy kingdom come. Thy will be done on earth, as it is in heaven. Give us this day our daily bread. And forgive us our debts as we forgive our debtors. And lead us not into temptation, but deliver us from evil";

The purpose: "For Thine is the kingdom and the power and the glory forever."

The credentials are in the Person who taught us the prayer. No matter how often you look at this prayer, no matter how often you pray this prayer, no matter how much you study this prayer or how deeply you lose yourself in its thoughts, you cannot get away from it — it is perfect. Not a single idle word is in it; yet all possible petitions are included.

The Bible is full of prayers and in reality is the source of all prayer, for whatever we know of prayer and of the efficacy of prayer and of the way of prayer we have learned from the Bible. But to make an exhaustive study of the prayers of the Bible and to do them justice would demand a separate essay — or better yet, a volume.

We have a rich treasure store of prayers in the collects of the church. They are known as collects because in them the petitions of the people are collected. "In the early church the priest would bid the people to pray for some special purpose. There would follow a time of silence during which each person prayed in his heart. Then the priest would collect all their prayers and offer them to God in a spoken prayer. Thus these summarizing prayers of the priest came to be called collects." (Garrett, p. 22)

Many of these collects of the church follow the same outline which we discern in the Lord's Prayer. Take the Collect for Purity, a prayer which is familiar to many people and perfect in form. Analyzing it, we have —

The address: "Almighty God";

The descriptive clause: "Unto whom all hearts are open, all desires known, and from whom no secrets are hid";

The petition: "Cleanse the thoughts of our hearts by the inspiration of Thy Holy Spirit";

The purpose: "That we may perfectly love Thee and worthily magnify Thy holy name";

The ending (which carries our credentials): "Through Jesus Christ, our Lord."

Needless to say, not all prayers need follow this perfect outline in order to be perfect prayers. In times of danger and distress we have the prayer of Psalm 70: "Make haste, O God, to deliver me; make haste to help me, O Lord. Let them be ashamed and confounded that seek after my soul; let them be turned backward and put to confusion that desire my hurt. Let them be turned back for a reward of their shame that say, Aha, aha! Let all those that seek Thee rejoice and be glad in Thee; and let such as love Thy salvation say continually, Let God be magnified. But I am poor and needy; make haste unto me, O God; Thou art my Help and my Deliverer; O Lord, make no tarrying." Or the briefer prayer of the disciples: "Lord, save us; we perish!" (Matthew 8:25); or that of Peter: "Lord, save me!" (Matthew 14:30). At the hour of death, when the time is hastening and the struggle is deep and prayer does so much to quiet the soul, we may pray as did David: "Into Thine hand I commit my spirit; Thou hast redeemed me, O Lord God of truth" (Psalm 31:5); or as did the Savior:

"Father, into Thy hands I commend My spirit" (Luke 23:46); or as did Stephen: "Lord Jesus, receive my spirit." (Acts 7:59)

Formal prayers are not stereotyped, not even the childlike prayer, which the Spirit teaches us and by reason of His indwelling prays with us, "Abba, Father." On the contrary, everyone will be greatly benefited by the study and the use of formal prayers.

POSTURE; VOICE

If once we have learned how to pray, the posture of the pray-er is of little import. It is the heart and the thought and the intent that is all-important. Whether we kneel or sit or lie or stand or walk or prostrate ourselves, whether we fold our hands or keep them busy, whether we bow our heads or look upward will depend largely upon the mood, upon the custom, upon the place, and upon the circumstances.

As to the voice in which we speak our prayers, again we need not worry about what is proper. When others are present, it is, of course, necessary that we speak distinctly enough for them to hear what we are saying. Monotonous mumbling, wholly devoid of emotion, as well as the opposite, unctuous, excessive modulation, interferes with the sanctity of the prayer. God wants His people to draw nigh unto Him with their hearts. (Matthew 15:8)

The Kinds of Prayer

We have come now to the point where we may study the various kinds of prayer.

Adoration is the loftiest form of prayer. It was the first prayer of the angels; for when God laid the foundations of the earth, "the morning stars sang together, and all the sons of God shouted for joy." (Job 38:7)

Whom we adore we admire; and yet adoration transcends admiration, for adoration is based upon the holiest and purest kind of love. It is the chief requirement of the Law of God and a requirement which the Gospel gives us the ability to fulfill. "Thou shalt love the Lord thy God with all thy heart and with all thy soul and with all thy mind" (Matthew 22:37). "It is a blending of love with the fervent desire that all the world should know and magnify the glory of the Lord." (Hastings, p. 55)

A beautiful prayer of adoration is the "Gloria in Excelsis" and its natural application in the Christmas prayer. "O Thou great and glorious Redeemer, who art Wonderful, Counselor, the Mighty God, the Everlasting Father, the Prince of Peace, we praise Thee, we bless Thee, we worship Thee, we glorify Thee, we give thanks to Thee for Thy great glory, O Lord God, Lamb of God, the only-begotten Son Jesus Christ, God of God, Light of Light, very God of very God, King of kings and Lord of lords, Emmanuel, God with us! For Thou only art holy; Thou only art the Lord; Thou only, O Christ, with the Holy Ghost, art most high in the glory of God the Father." And then comes the second paragraph: "But chiefly at this time do we adore Thee for leaving the glory which Thou hadst with the Father before the world began.

91

We know Thy grace, O Lord Jesus Christ, that, though Thou wast rich, yet for our sakes Thou didst become poor that we through Thy poverty might be made rich." Here we have the reason, the enkindling cause of our adoration: "We love Him because He first loved us." (1 John 4:19)

Adoration, it has been said, is the homage of the creature to the Creator. And we do indeed bow in lowliness before the Creator, who fashioned the stars and scattered abroad the mighty constellations! Ah, yes! But beside the crib of Christ we come upon a God far more gracious, far more divine, far more adorable! That is adoration!

We have reason to excel the angels in adoration. The angels in their innocence can say, "Holy, holy, holy is the Lord of hosts; the whole earth is full of His glory" (Isaiah 6:3); and the saints will one day join them in saying, "Worthy is the Lamb that was slain to receive power and riches and wisdom and strength and honor and glory and blessing" (Revelation 5:12); but only the saints — not the angels, only the saints — redeemed now, and redeemed then, stumbling now, victorious then, can say, "Unto Him that loved us and washed us from our sins in His own blood and hath made us kings and priests unto God and His Father, to Him be glory and dominion forever and ever. Amen" (Revelation 1:5, 6). That is adoration!

More often should we think adoringly, magnificently about God, for by such prayerful exercise we draw closer to God.

Jehovah, let me now adore Thee
For where is there a God such, Lord, as Thou?
With songs I fain would come before Thee;
Oh, Let Thy Holy Spirit teach me now
To praise Thee in His name through whom alone
Our songs can please Thee, Through Thy blessed Son!
(Crasselius)

To the great One in Three
Eternal praises be
Hence evermore!
His sov'reign majesty
May we in glory see
And to eternity
Love and adore! (Author unknown)

CONFESSION

God is so great; and we are so infinitesimally small! God is so holy; and we are so full of sin! We feel the need for penitential prayers — prayers of confession.

In confession the pray-er's keenest consciousness is of his sin, his guilt, his unworthiness. "I acknowledge my transgressions; and my sin is ever before me," laments David in Psalm 51. I am conscious of my sin as contrasted with the holiness of God. I am conscious of my guilt as contrasted with the innocence of God. I am conscious of my utter unworthiness as contrasted with the large expectation the worthy Judge Eternal had in me as man, the very crown of His creation. And in the awareness of my personal sin, in the acuteness of my personal guilt, and in the acknowledgment of my personal unworthiness I cry, "Against Thee, Thee only, have I sinned and done this evil in Thy sight." (Psalm 51:4)

93

Sunday after Sunday I join my fellow worshipers in the Confession of Sins: "We poor sinners confess unto Thee that we are by nature sinful and unclean and that we have sinned against Thee by thought, word, and deed"; and in the confessional preparatory to Holy Communion, "O almighty God, merciful Father, I, a poor, miserable sinner, confess unto Thee all my sins and iniquities with which I have ever offended Thee and justly deserved Thy temporal and eternal punishment. But I am heartily sorry for them and sincerely repent of them." There is something peculiarly solemn in this united confession of sins. Differences of social position are lost sight of as we humbly bow before the Maker of us all. "There is no difference; for all have sinned and come short of the glory of God." (Romans 3:22, 23)

But is general confession enough for the good of my soul? Being general, does it remain just that, general? Does it particularize my sins enough? The needle points prick; yes, they do; but with so many needle points packed together, is there not a possibility that instead of a series of stings I will feel only a little roughness?

To keep my conscience sharp and the consciousness of my sinfulness alive I need to examine myself in a private audience with God. My confession must be severely personal.

Mentally I make a list of my sins. I examine myself according to the Ten Commandments. I consider my station in life, whether I am a father, mother, son, daughter, employer, employee; whether I have been disobedient, unfaithful, lazy; whether I have grieved any person by word or deed; whether I have cheated, stolen, or wasted my time and energy or possessions. I try to determine why I did what I did or failed to do what I should have done. I look at the ugliness of my sins without trying to excuse them and try to see them as God sees them. I remember that my sins are never the fault of someone else. They are never the result of some untoward circumstance. They are flaws within my own character. Other people and certain circumstances may be a contributing cause, aggravating my weakness, but they are never the cause of my sins. I am the guilty one. "God, be merciful to me, a sinner" (Luke 18:13). "Have mercy upon me, O God, according to Thy loving-kindness; according unto the multitude of Thy tender mercies blot out my transgressions. Wash me thoroughly from mine iniquity, and cleanse me from my sin" (Psalm 51:1, 2). "I pray Thee of Thy boundless mercy and for the sake of the holy, innocent, bitter sufferings and death of Thy beloved Son, Jesus Christ, to be gracious and merciful to me, a poor sinful being." In deep sorrow over sins committed and faults unknown, I penitently confess my transgressions before God and reach out for a forgiveness which is ill-deserved but freely promised.

In the first of his Ninety-five Theses Luther writes: "When our Lord and Master Jesus Christ says, Repent, He means that the whole life of believers upon earth should be a constant and perpetual repentance," and in his explanation of the Third Article of the Apostles' Creed he sets forth that the Holy Spirit "daily and richly forgives all sins to me and all be-

95

lievers." These words are not inspired, but they faithfully reflect the truth revealed in Scripture that "the blood of Jesus Christ, His Son, cleanseth us from all sin. If we say that we have no sin, we deceive ourselves, and the truth is not in us. If we confess our sins, He is faithful and just to forgive us our sins and to cleanse us from all unrighteousness." (1 John 1:7-9)

SUPPLICATION — INCLUDING PRAYER
FOR PHYSICAL HEALING

The penitential prayer, then, includes a supplication, for not only do we acknowledge our sinfulness and unworthiness, but we also plead for pardon and forgiveness.

The prayer of supplication, however, includes more than a plea for pardon and forgiveness; it includes any and all petitions for pardon, grace, or any other blessing we may need or desire. Perhaps most of our prayers fall into this category.

Let us never disparage the privilege of petition. It is God-given. "Ask," says Jesus in His Sermon on the Mount, "and it shall be given unto you" (Matthew 7:7). "Ask." True it is that prayer is not merely asking but also any form of communion with God in adoration, confession, praise, and thanksgiving; nevertheless the primary meaning of prayer is petition, and we do not really know how to pray until we have learned how to ask.

What may we ask God for? The simple answer is "Everything." Nothing is too momentous, and nothing is too trivial to be remembered before God in prayer.

No department of life should be excluded from the sphere of prayer, neither the spiritual nor the mental nor the physical. The Lord wants it so, for He is concerned about the details of our life. The very hairs of our head are all numbered (cp. Matthew 10:30). All our wants and desires and therefore all the wants and desires of others can be brought to God's attention. "In everything," writes St. Paul, "by prayer and supplication with thanksgiving let your requests be made known unto God" (Philippians 4:6). There is nothing too big for the power of God, and nothing too small for His love.

How great the condescension of our God! "Who is like unto the Lord, our God, who dwelleth on high, who humbleth Himself to behold the things that are in heaven and in the earth! He raiseth up the poor out of the dust and lifteth the needy out of the dunghill" (Psalm 113:5, 6). There is no desire, no plan, no enterprise, no act, no relationship in life, in which we are not dependent on divine guidance, help, and blessing; and "as life wears on and brings out its trials and reveals its uncertainties," we are "more and more thrown back on God as the One who knows us, who fully sympathizes with us, and who can really help us" (Hastings, p. 91). And the help is so readily available. "Ask," He says (Matthew 7:7). "Call." (Psalm 50:15)

Naturally, when we make our requests, we must observe the proper order, the order which Jesus indicates in His Prayer. He bids us think first of God and of His holiness, of the spread of His kingdom here on earth, and of His heavenly will being done at all

97

times and in all places. Only then follow personal petitions, and of these, three are concerned with the removal of spiritual obstacles which would separate us from God: forgiveness of sin, rescue from temptation, and deliverance from evil. One, and one only, is devoted to our temporal welfare, and that one in its simplest form, "Give us this day our daily bread" (cf. Hastings, pp. 89f.). The proper order, then, is: "Seek ye first the kingdom of God and His righteousness, and all these things shall be added unto you." (Matthew 6:33)

But do not let anyone deprive you of the privilege of asking for anything that you may need or that your heart may desire. Asking is still the primary meaning of prayer.

However, when we make our requests, we must remember that God is in the heavens and that He knows our necessities and our wants even before we ask and that we must therefore not insult Him by using vain repetitions, as the heathen do, or think that we shall be heard for our much speaking (Matthew 6:7). After all, we have no reason to doubt the Lord's ability to hear or His readiness to answer.

And let's wait for an answer. Let's give God a chance to answer. Prayer is a dialog. We must listen in silence for an answer and not do all the talking. We must learn the simple lesson which Eli taught little Samuel. "If He call thee . . . thou shalt say, 'Speak, Lord; for Thy servant heareth' " (1 Samuel 3:9). Listen for an answer. Wait for an answer.

It will happen more than once that God will not give us what we ask for. After all, He sees farther than we do; and if in our ignorance we ask for something that will do us more harm than good, God the Father will give, not the thing that we ask for but the thing that we should and would have asked for, could we have seen as far as He sees.

Now, with God at the receiving end of our petitions and ready to sift the harmful from the good, what's to hinder us by prayer and supplication with thanksgiving to let our requests be made known unto God in everything? (Philippians 4:6)

Even in sickness and health.

"In everything," says the apostle Paul. "Be careful for nothing, but in everything by prayer and supplication with thanksgiving let your requests be made known unto God" (Philippians 4:6). Is physical health included in that "everything"? Is physical health a legitimate subject of prayer? Luther thought so. He listed physical health as an important item under "daily bread." Wrote he in explanation of the Fourth Petition and in answer to the question, "What is meant by daily bread?" "Everything" — again that word "everything" — "Everything that belongs to the support and wants of the body," and then proceeded to include "health" in that category. Why should we now hesitate to include it? That we do hesitate, it seems to me, is borne out by a special request for a separate discussion of prayer for physical healing. I say this not in censure. I wish only to analyze the difficulty that lies before us. Doubting minds! Hesitant hearts! Spirits that lack the desired confidence!

There is implied in the preceding statement what may be considered an unfair accusation. However,

I would not care to accuse any one of you of a lack of confidence in God's ability to heal disease. You have all heard His claim, "I am the Lord that healeth thee" (Exodus 15:26). You would not doubt that claim. Why, then, the hesitant hearts? Do we perhaps hesitate because we are afraid of being regarded as extremists if we rely too much on God for healing?

After all, there is such a phenomenon as divine healing. Come along with me to Bethesda, and see for yourself. (John 5:1-14)

Bethesda, the House of Mercy, was so named because the building, which consisted of five porches, or porticoes, had been built around a pool by that name. In these five porches lay a multitude of invalids, blind, lame, paralyzed, anxiously "waiting for the moving [the bubbling up] of the water" in the pool. This was a phenomenon peculiar to this pool. Those who do not believe in miracles ascribe it to a siphonlike action caused by an underground spring. The evangelist, however, attributed it to the fact that an angel came down to the pool at certain times and disturbed the water. The first person who entered the water after its disturbance would become well, no matter what his disease might be.

On a certain feast day Jesus visited this House of Mercy. As He walked among the misery-laden cots and pallets, His eyes rested on a wasted and weary form. Tenderly He stooped over and asked the sufferer, "Wilt thou be made whole?" The invalid had no idea who it was that was speaking to him, and wearily he explained, as he had, no doubt, often done

100

before for the benefit of other sympathetic inquisitors, "Naturally I want to be healed; but what's the use? Look at me. Can't you see that in my condition I cannot get down to the water fast enough? Every time the water bubbles up, either someone else steps in ahead of me, or some friend carries another person down before me. I have no one who is concerned about me. I have given up hope long ago." And then He whose mighty power is never bound and who is ever the Help of the helpless simply said, "Rise, take up thy bed, and walk." "And immediately the man was made whole and took up his bed and walked." A stupendous act! And so little fanfare!

When Jesus had healed the man, He quietly withdrew Himself and disappeared in the crowd. He still had something to say to the man whom He had healed, but He felt that it would be better to say it at another time. After the first surge of emotion had passed and the crowd would no longer be shouting and the lowering Pharisees would be gone, He would be able the better to impress upon the man a truth even more important than the fact of being healed of an affliction. Sometime later He managed to find the man in the temple. There He gave him the message: "Behold, thou art made whole; sin no more, lest a worse thing come unto thee."

There is, indeed, such a phenomenon as divine healing; and physical healing is, therefore, a legitimate subject of prayer; but the phenomenon of divine healing, as well as the subject of prayer for physical healing, does not stand alone. The subject brings in its wake a host of questions, the answers to which have a bearing on the subject and some of which over-shadow the subject in importance.

Earlier, when speaking of the scientific difficulties in the way of prayer, I quoted what we have come to recognize as the objection of the materialistic mind: "We know that health and disease are the result of physiological laws, which absolutely determine that one man shall live and another die and that it is there-fore unreasonable and even unnecessary to ask God to intervene when our doctors have a supply of won-der drugs which will produce the necessary chemical reaction that shall arrest the disease and restore health." This objection looms surprisingly large, now that the Lord Jesus Christ is no longer visibly present with us to inspire our confidence by His physical contact.

To the one who raises this objection, if he desires at all to believe in the efficacy of prayer for physical health, the difficulty undoubtedly is that modern sci-ence and the art of healing seem highly efficient, while prayer for healing seems to be an uncertain quantity.

The science of healing was not always so efficient as it is today. This science has come a long, long way. At the time of the early Christian church medical sci-ence, to mention one branch, hardly deserved the name. What was recognized as scientific was a strange medley of quackery and witchcraft; the slender under-standing of human physiology and of drugs was more than neutralized by the trickery and the superstition with which it was associated so that medical treat-ment — then more so than now — often tended to aggravate the disease rather than to cure it. With such a condition of things prevailing it was undoubtedly wiser to induce a patient by means of prayer to fortify his will to combat the disease and the physician rather than to encourage him to rely upon the bungling medical aid of the day. Prayer did, perforce, play the larger role, a factor which, no doubt, influenced the practice of the early Christian church which is indicated in the exhortation of St. James: "Is any sick among you? Let him call for the elders of the church, and let them pray over him, anointing him with oil in the name of the Lord, and the prayer of faith shall save the sick." (James 5:14, 15)

Has the science of healing now progressed so far and become so efficient as to make prayer unnecessary or at best an auxiliary aid in the curing of physical ills, a standby, perhaps, upon which we can fall back as a last resort when all medical or other therapeutic treatments fail, a haven of desperation? If it were that, and only that, we would still appreciate the privilege.

But is prayer meant to play a secondary role to medicine or therapy? The idolatry of modern science might wish to have it so. But shall our faith be tyrannized by this modern idolatry? We are, indeed, impressed by the science of healing; yet, on second thought, you will agree with me that there are many treatments in common use at our modern hospitals and clinics which have behind them far less evidence of effectiveness than the practice of prayer for the sick. Furthermore, you will agree that if prayer works as a last resort it will work with equal ease as a first resort.

Medicine and prayer were never meant to be in conflict, as little as science and faith were ever meant to be in conflict. There is here a large area for co-operation.

Medicine is God's gift as much as the sun that shines upon us and the bread that we eat. We pray for daily bread, and God opens His bountiful hand to satisfy our desire. We pray for physical healing, and God reaches out His sympathetic hand to supply us with the medicine that we need. That in each case He works through intermediaries does not in the least detract from His glory. It is still He who is the Lord that healeth us.

Many of our temporal prayers are anticipated by God, who lives in eternity, and their answer is guaranteed in God's decree of preservation: "Be fruitful and multiply, and replenish the earth, and subdue it" (Genesis 1:28). God has contributed mightily to the great discoveries of science; in fact, without His contribution there would have been nothing for science to discover. What else is a scientific discovery but the discovery of another one of God's bounties and of its use? All the bounties are there. By scientific discoveries man has been able gradually to "subdue" them and to use them for his purposes.

This holds true in the sphere of the science of healing as well as in any other sphere. God has provided mankind with many glorious gifts of nature for the healing of the body, for the curing of disease, or for alleviating pain — and every one of these is an instance of divine healing. Penicillin and sulfa drugs are supposed to be something quite new. But yeast

104

mold has always had the same healing properties, and the component elements of sulfanilamide have had from creation the healing powers newly discovered. The same may be said of all drugs or herbs or methods which have been discovered by science. They are not something new; they are merely new discoveries of God's gifts for healing. And God expects us to use these gifts for our physical well-being.

In consequence, the obligation is laid upon us to seek the answer to our prayers by co-operating with God's bountiful endowments as contributed through medical or therapeutical science. In other words, we are prayerfully to use the medicines and therapies that are available, keeping in mind, however, that they do have their limitations and also that their use does not at all rule out the need for prayer. There were times when even our Lord did not hesitate to use external aids, as when He applied clay to the eyes of the blind man; and even in the church of the apostolic age the oil applied to the sick one, to which St. James refers, had a therapeutic as well as a ritualistic purpose. Never should we think that the need for prayer has been eliminated by modern science. It is even recognized by physicians, though many of them may ascribe the evident effectiveness of prayer to autosuggestion.

We would prefer to call it faith healing. And faith healing does play a prominent part in our prayers for physical healing. But what is faith healing?

Faith healing is more than autosuggestion, though autosuggestion may play a role in the healing. Faith healing is more than the principle of psychiatry that the spirit exercises a dominant influence over the body, though its effective result may be similar; for the buoyant faith and the determined will of the individual have at times achieved what external remedies failed to do. A wise physician knows this and uses the principle to good advantage. His smile is often as good as his medicine, for it inspires hope and confidence. At times he relies more on this confidence which he generates in the patient than on the drugs which he injects.

And now I ask you, what can inspire hope and generate confidence more than prayer? This is the reason why the door of the sickroom is seldom closed to the pastor. By prayer we come to God, realizing that "He knoweth our frame." He can diagnose our condition as no doctor can. His understanding is infinite, His love perfect, His power unlimited. We can approach Him with the confidence that He who made our body is most capable of remaking it and healing it. This is more than autosuggestion. It is faith healing. It is born not merely of faith in ourselves nor of confidence in an intermediary but of faith in God. And it is in perfect harmony with the principle of co-operation in prayer.

Applying this principle, we conclude that as we are obliged to utilize whatever material healing aids are at hand so we are privileged to ask God for a blessing upon these aids and upon us. Someone has said that "it is not really absurd to suggest that drugs and no prayer may be almost as foolish as prayer and no drugs." However, if a choice were to be made between drugs and prayer, might it not be wiser and safer to choose prayer? Drugs may be dangerous; prayer never is. But God does not require us to make the choice. "Prayer" and "oil," says St. James. Use both! Prayer and medicine, or medicine and prayer.

So far we have treated this subject of prayer for physical healing from a somewhat selfish angle. We have not yet met the question of prayer in behalf of our sick friends. Can our prayers procure healing for others who are suffering? The answer and the application, it seems to me, varies not at all from the prayers which we may pray in our own behalf. It is the same God who is at the receiving end of our prayers.

Let us try to analyze the situation.

Here our prayers take on the nature of an intercession, an area which we shall explore in the following section. Intercession presupposes concern; and another man's concern is a powerful tonic for the spirit of man. It is certainly within the realm of possibility that our prayers for the sick, concerned as they are with the afflicted and linked to the infinite power of God, should have such an effect on the spirit of the patient, conscious or unconscious or both, that the whole psychical atmosphere, which his spirit is breathing, is changed, if not charged. The depressed spirit becomes optimistic; the defeated spirit finds new hope; the worn-out spirit receives new courage; and all these have a tremendous effect on the physical condition of the body. Are these psychiatric phenomena too strange to understand or to credit?

Closely allied to this possibility is the fact that our prayers in behalf of the sick can and do stimulate the faith of the one prayed for. This is a far cry from advocating psychical healing through the mediation of a mesmeric personality or a supposedly superendowed clergyman. That would be creating a separate medical priestcraft, a spiritual monstrosity wholly foreign to the spirit of the New Testament. There is no separate priestcraft in the New Testament. We are all — clergy and laity, and laity as well as clergy — priests before the Lord; and we can all exercise the magnetic touch of faith, whether our name be Ronald, Richard, or Robert. By our prayers in behalf of the sick we can mightily strengthen his confidence in God, so that in the day of recovery we can say to him, as Jesus once said to the blind man of Jericho, "Thy faith hath made thee whole." (Mark 10:52)

But apart from this, apart from any influence which we by our prayers may be able to exercise on the sick, we can also expect God through our intercessory prayers to focus the rays of divine healing on the diseased and in response to our prayers to give direct healing even at a distance. To deny so evident a truth would be to deny the love and the compassion and the power of God.

But if God is full of compassion and all-powerful, why does He need our prayers? He doesn't need our prayers. However, the sick need our prayers, for God sometimes does not choose to unleash His healing power until we pray for it. A father once brought his afflicted son to the disciples of Jesus that they should cast out the dumb and deaf spirit that afflicted him but they failed in their attempt. Baffled, they later on asked Jesus, "Why could not we cast him out?" And Jesus answered them, "This kind can come forth by nothing but by prayer and fasting" (Mark 9:28, 29). We should not take intercessory prayer in behalf of the sick lightly. Often it spells the difference between despair and hope, between sickness and health, between death and life. To say more than this just now would be to anticipate many of the statements which are to follow in the next section.

That prayer sometimes fails to obtain healing no more discredits its value than the fact that the doctor sometimes fails in his efforts should discredit the science of healing. We must, however, beware of thinking that success or failure is due to caprice or deliberate prejudice on the part of God. God is love, and perfect love is wholly trustworthy to do what is just and what is best. And there is abundant evidence to show that when men trustingly turn to God in prayer, even though their prayer for deliverance be not granted, they receive strength for their trial and are quite content. The experience of St. Paul remains the classic example. "For this thing [the thorn in the flesh] I besought the Lord thrice, that it might depart from me. And He said unto me, My grace is sufficient for thee, for My strength is made perfect in weakness. Most gladly therefore will I rather glory in my infirmities that the power of Christ may rest upon me. Therefore I take pleasure in infirmities, in reproaches, in necessities, in persecutions, in distresses for Christ's sake; for when I am weak, then am I strong" (2 Corinthians 12:8-10). Certainly we ought never to lose sight of the principle that as we pray for physical healing it is incumbent upon us as children of God to pray in the spirit of submissiveness.

As Christians we must also keep in mind that healing in answer to prayer is never an end in itself and that divine healing in itself is not an article of faith by which the church stands or falls. To believe that there is such a phenomenon as divine healing is a far cry from saying that a person can't be a full-fledged Christian unless he has experienced divine healing or that a church does not have the full Gospel unless it gives the subject of divine healing the central place in its doctrine and practice. We ought never hesitate when asked which is the greater, healing of body or healing of soul. The body is but an envelope, a temporary tabernacle, and sickness and death of the body are only matters of time, whereas all that concerns the soul concerns eternity and determines also the eternal destiny of the body. We must not overemphasize divine healing. To read the words of Jesus is to be assured of this. Time after time He gave the same admonition to those whom He had healed: "Don't go talking about it too much." He did this to guard against the danger that the crowds whom He longed to win would come to Him as the Healer of their bodies rather than the Savior of their souls. Of course, He is both, but He desires primarily to be the Savior of our souls; for unless our souls be healed and saved, the healing of the body will be of no avail. Untouched, there would still remain the root of all diseases — sin.

Discouraging as it may sound, there is a direct relationship between sickness and sin.

Whether we walk through the wards of an institution, where the results of degenerate living and

110

reckless dissipation are sometimes directly evident, or whether we sit at the bedside of an afflicted God-fearing person, the cause of sickness, illness, pain, debility, and suffering of body is always sin. If it were not for sin, there would be no sickness.

It must even be said that certain sins entail special painful and dreadful results. Jesus said to the man at Bethesda who had been bedridden for thirty-eight years, "Behold, thou art made whole; sin no more lest a worse thing come unto thee" (John 5:14). Thirty-eight years ago he had sinned — sinned in a way his conscience at once painfully recalled, sinned so as to wreck his life in consequence of sin.

However, this does not mean that every sickness of short or long duration is directly traceable to some specific sin. In the case of the man born blind Jesus would not allow His disciples to infer that his affliction had been caused by a specific sin. (John 9:1-3)

But the truth remains: sickness and all physical ills would never have come into the world at all if sin had not come first. God created man in His own image, holy and perfect. He placed man into the Garden of Eden and gave him a moral test in connection with the tree of the knowledge of good and evil. "In the day that thou eatest thereof, thou shalt surely die" (Genesis 2:17). Man disregarded this command, and the process of death set in, for sin began to generate sicknesses and ills and pains and, finally, death of the body.

In view of this, to be sick is not the worst thing that can happen to a person. Jesus told the man who had been healed, "Sin no more lest a worse thing come unto thee." Many think that, when a severe and long illness comes upon them, nothing could be worse. They are wrong. There is something far worse — eternal suffering in hell, the result of sins unforgiven. To save us from that, there is no Helper but Jesus. He, and He alone, is the Great Physician, who can prevent eternal death.

Our sicknesses and our frailties, then, are to remind us of our sinfulness and of our dire need of a Savior from sin, who alone can heal our souls and save us for eternity.

Never, therefore, should we forget that the forgiveness of sins is more important than the healing of the body, and prayer for spiritual healing more important than prayer for physical healing. If we lose sight of this, we shall be running with the hares of faith while chasing with the hounds of materialism. We shall be ignoring the fundamental fact about disease — human sin, of which our ills are the offspring. Purely physical remedies are merely palliatives, which may for a while arrest or even cure a specific disease but fail to eradicate disease as such. We need the forgiveness of sin. This is our foremost need, whether we be sick or well.

Thank God, in Christ Jesus we have redemption through His blood, even the forgiveness of sin. "Bless the Lord, O my soul, and forget not all His benefits" — and now notice the order in which the psalmist mentions His benefits — "who forgiveth all thine iniquities, who healeth all thy diseases" (Psalm 103:2, 3). Saint James also calls attention to the primary need for forgiveness, though he brings it as an afterthought, as a reminder of its paramount importance even in connection with prayers for physical healing. "Is any sick among you? Let him call for the elders of the church, and let them pray over him, anointing him with oil in the name of the Lord, and the prayer of faith shall save the sick, and the Lord shall raise him up; and if he have committed sins, they shall be forgiven him." (James 5:14, 15)

When we therefore pray for physical healing, either for ourselves or for others, we should offer our prayers with the recognition that diseases and death are for us not unmitigated evils, much as we might dread them or wish to be free of them, "for we know that the whole creation groaneth and travaileth in pain together until now. And not only they, but ourselves also, which have the first fruits of the Spirit, even we ourselves groan within ourselves, waiting for the adoption, to wit, the redemption of our body" (Romans 8:22, 23). Our body, in its corrupt form, is but a temporary tabernacle for our soul, a transitory shell in which our personality is to develop until the time comes for the laying aside of this tabernacle to give our Savior the opportunity to work a miracle of restoration and to change our vile bodies that they may be fashioned like unto His glorious body (Philippians 3:21). Prayer for physical healing is therefore not intended to abolish the effects of diseases but to lessen them temporarily; it is not intended to perpetuate life but perchance to prolong it, if such be God's will. The time will come when we shall gladly say: "Lord, now lettest Thou Thy servant depart in peace, according to Thy word; for mine eyes have seen Thy salvation" (Luke 2:29, 30). If we do not look forward to that time with anticipation, we have no right ever to pray the Lord's Prayer to its end. "Our Father . . . deliver us from evil."

We could well conclude this section here, were it not for the fact that this privilege of praying for physical healing is so liable to gross abuse. Early in the church's history the practice of psychical healing degenerated into a fraudulent conspiracy for robbing the credulous. Superstition was fostered, saints' bones and other supposed miracle-working relics were faked, healing shrines came into vogue. The practice gained a tenacious hold on the people and was justified by its advocates under the pretense of faith and was erroneously called faith healing, or even divine healing.

Of late there has been appearing on television a program to which my attention was called because of the concern which it has caused some of our good and faithful Christians. It is a program which features a man who claims to be able by the power of God to heal all manner of sickness by the touch of his hand or even by the influence that is emitted over the frequencies by his outstretched hand.

What do I think of the program? Since my attention was called to it, I have watched it a few times. I was not impressed. On television even the most stupendous phenomenon can be staged. The program, therefore, proves nothing; and so far as I am concerned, I give it no credence. Whether the program has ever done any good I have no way of knowing. I do know that some Christians have been greatly disturbed by it. There is a dangerous logic propounded by the program. The import is that if your faith is strong enough, you, too, can be healed of your sickness as the man prays for you. The Christian watches. If he is sick — or has been sick and ailing for years — he yearns for healing, naturally. The promise of the program gives him a momentary glimmer of hope. The program fades from the screen, and the poor man has experienced no healing. Do you see what such an experience can do to a Christian's faith if his faith happens to be weak? His faith can easily be undermined and even founder, as he utterly despairs of being a Christian. This may be an extreme situation, but it is a distinct possibility.

But apart from the television program, which is admittedly severely edited so that each and every healing session comes through without a single failure, what of the actual healing session under the tent? Whether I am now the person qualified to give a trustworthy evaluation may be questionable. I have never been there to observe. I can only judge by what has been published and has come to my attention.

It is admitted by this self-styled healer that he has not been able to heal in every instance and that he does have his failures; but he also claims that this should not discredit him as a healer. His admission is commendable, and his claim might be fair. However, a closer study of the successes reveals that these are scored in the field of the neurotic and therefore coincide closely with what we know about healing in general. Many a disease is psychosomatic. More people than ever are victims of neuroses. These neuroses would be likely to yield to a mesmeric personality. Under the exhilarating stimulus of a new neurotic experience the neurotic disorder might even disappear entirely, and the person is "healed." There is nothing miraculous about it; an elementary principle of psychiatry has been applied.

But what of the testimony of those who say they have actually been healed of a physical affliction? Whether the claim rests on truth or not, I have no way of telling. It is a claim I can neither verify nor deny; however, I can most sincerely doubt it.

It has been brought to my attention — the locale is in a northern Wisconsin community — that certain people who were afflicted went and apparently were healed of their affliction and returned and felt well for the time being. After a little while, however, the old affliction returned. The exhilarating stimulus may well have served as a palliative, much like the injection of a drug until the effects wear off. The stimulus served to buoy up their spirits to such a degree that they were able temporarily to conquer the effects of the disease without, however, affecting the disease. Imagine their tragic disillusionment! We must seek to guide them back to spiritual sanity.

Another example. This time the locale is even closer to home. In contrast to Jesus, who was able to heal all manner of disease, this publicity-hungry faith healer must resort to a safety device to improve his batting average. The applicants are carefully screened, and the "incurables" are not invited to approach. What else did you expect?

116

And now I wish to suggest to you a simple method by which you may test the "healer's" effectiveness — and save yourself the expense of a long and fruitless trip. He lays himself open to the test. If you actually believe there might be something to this business, take him up on it. The next time you watch the program and he at the close of the program stretches his extended fingers through the television screen to overshadow your faces as you sit in your easy chair on the opposite side of the room and invites you to touch the television set as he prays for you right where you are, so that you, too, may be healed, take him up on it! If you have never noticed it before, you will notice it then, that the television set, after having been turned on for half an hour, is warm.

Shall we conclude?

Christians will do well to remember that Jesus' power to heal is still unlimited — limited only by His own omniscient foreknowledge of what is best for us. Surely we will utilize every means that science can discover or devise to cure and alleviate sickness and infirmity, always remembering that a loving God has put these healing gifts into His created world, remembering, too, that they have their limitations. And where these natural means are limited, we will surely also storm the heart of Jesus and plead: "I would be healed," knowing that His power to heal is unlimited. However, when we so pray we shall not forget to add, "Nevertheless not my will, but Thine, be done," knowing that He in His loving concern for us may have chosen a cross for us, but knowing, too, that even so He will never afflict us needlessly.

One more thing I would like to point out. We must never permit the phenomenon of divine healing to become a touchstone of our faith; for if we did, then we would imply that only those who are healed and only those who are well can be regarded as Christians — a view which the Bible nowhere teaches.

If the Lord in His loving concern heals us of our bodily ills, we, as Christians, are deeply grateful and dedicate our restored health to His service. And if the Lord in His loving wisdom decides that we shall bear our affliction longer, we, as Christians, humbly submit to His will — and also dedicate ourselves to His service — knowing that also our afflictions will, in keeping with His loving concern, serve a purpose. Afflictions do carry a message of divine love. Remember the words of the apostle to the Hebrews: "Ye have forgotten the exhortation which speaketh unto you as unto children: My son, despise not thou the chastening of the Lord, nor faint when thou art rebuked of Him; for whom the Lord loveth he chasteneth, and scourgeth every son whom he receiveth. If ye endure chastening, God dealeth with you as with sons; for what son is he whom the father chasteneth not? But if ye be without chastisement, whereof all are partakers, then are ye bastards and not sons. Furthermore we have had fathers of our flesh which corrected us, and we gave them reverence; shall we not much rather be in subjection unto the Father of spirits and live? For they verily for a few days chastened us after their own pleasure; but He for our profit that we might be partakers of His holiness. Now, no chastening for the present seemeth to be joyous, but grievous;

nevertheless afterward it yieldeth the peaceable fruit of righteousness unto them which are exercised thereby." (Hebrews 12:5-11)

The touchstone of our Christianity is not whether we be well or whether we be sick or whether we be healed. The touchstone of our Christianity is whether we have in our sad condition turned to Jesus Christ, the Son of God, as our Savior, who alone can heal us from the root of all diseases — sin. This is the touchstone: "Believe on the Lord Jesus Christ, and thou shalt be saved and thy house." (Acts 16:31)

INTERCESSION

We must never let our prayers degenerate into selfishness by narrowing them to ourselves and to our own wants. Naturally we are concerned about our own duties, our own work, our own needs, our own spiritual growth, our own sorrows and trials; but as we think of these, let us not forget to look out of the window on our neighbor's rough path or sore struggle. "I exhort therefore," writes St. Paul, "that, first of all, supplications, prayers, intercessions, and giving of thanks be made for all men" (1 Timothy 2:1). Prayers of intercession are an important part of Christian living. God wants us to pray for others.

But what is the value of intercessory prayer? What good does it do? Though its full value lies beyond our ken, it, like mercy,

> . . . is twice blest;
> It blesseth him that gives and him that takes.
>> (Merchant of Venice, *Act IV, Scene 1*)

119

Intercessory prayer will influence the one who prays, for it will affect both his disposition and his inclination.

When one person sincerely prays for another person, he will be more kindly disposed toward that person. Take the case of a woman who prays, sincerely and lovingly prays, for the conversion of her husband. Her prayers may not be answered immediately. She continues to pray. It affects her disposition, makes her more Christlike, deepens her affection for her husband, and she becomes a better and better wife. Gradually her husband is influenced by her disposition and her behavior. The field has been prepared for the seed of the Gospel.

Again when a person sincerely prays for another person, he will be more inclined to do him good. Take the case of a Christian who prays, sincerely and lovingly prays, for his ailing neighbor. He will follow his prayer with a solicitous visit and with a readiness to help where help is needed. The sick neighbor is cheered. His spirit is lifted. Maybe it is just the tonic he needs for recovery. But even if he does not recover, his days will have become more cheerful.

But there is even more to intercessory prayer. It also has an effect on the person prayed for — even when unbeknown to him. This may seem passing strange, but, as Tennyson says,

> *More things are wrought by prayer*
> *Than this world dreams of.*

You remember the miracle of Jesus stilling the tempest on the Sea of Galilee. He was in the boat with His disciples. Have you ever given any thought to

120

"the other little ships" that were with Him? The men in those ships maybe never did find out just why their ships were not swamped by the waves and why the sudden calm. So it is with intercessory prayer. How often we ourselves may have been influenced for good, our twanging nerves calmed, some danger removed, some difficulty overcome because someone unbeknown to us was praying for us!

But how can I, a feeble, erring human being, through my prayer influence God for the good of someone else? I do not know; but this I do know, that I do not need to understand how intercessory prayer works to make use of it, no more than I need to know how electricity works before I can use it. Perhaps there is a current of love.

Our intercession is based on the intercession of Jesus Christ, who loves us with a love which cannot be measured. He is our great High Priest. His intercession avails for us before God the Father (Hebrews 7:25; 1 John 2:1). He has made us priests before God (Revelation 1:6). Now, when our intercessions coincide with His intercessions, or when His intercessions are added to ours, need we still ask, How can these things be?

For whom, then, should we intercede? St. Paul tells us, "For all men." (1 Timothy 2:1)

Naturally we will pray for the members of our family, mentioning them in our prayers, as their individual needs arise, by name. These are dear to us.

Certainly also we will pray for the church, the kingdom of God, of which we and the members of our family are members, or, if they be not, of which we desire them to be members. The church in our time stands in one of the most agonizing crises of its long history. The gates of hell are storming its very ramparts. The church will stand, surely it will, "for the gates of hell shall not prevail again it" (Matthew 16:18); but God wants us all to stand in the breach. Here is work which even the feeblest hands can do: pray. It is a contribution of paramount importance.

The church at home needs our prayers.

Here, whether we be the pastor or the pastured, we may well follow the example of St. Paul and pray for the members and for the membership of the church. How tenderly he remembers his friends and fellow laborers before the Mercy Seat! To the Thessalonian believers he writes that he is praying night and day that he might get to see them once more so that he might strengthen their faith; and he asks God to direct his way to them. He also intercedes for them that the Lord may increase their love toward one another and toward all men, so that in all things they may live lives that are a credit to their Christian calling (1 Thessalonians 3:10-13). Writing to them a second time, he says that he prays always for them that God would count them worthy of their calling, fulfill His good pleasure in them, and energize their work of faith, so that our Lord Jesus Christ might be glorified in them (2 Thessalonians 1:11, 12). He prays that the Lord Jesus Christ Himself and God, even our Father, might comfort their hearts and stablish them in every good word and work (2 Thessalonians 2:16, 17) and that the Lord might direct their hearts into the love of God and the patience of Christ

122

(2 Thessalonians 3:5). This same pattern of intercessory prayer is followed in his other epistles. Always
he makes intercession for the supreme and vital things.
He jots down, as it were, the great necessities of the
believers and spreads them out before the Mercy Seat.
We should do likewise.

In interceding for the church at home we should
not forget the office-bearers, the elders and the
trustees, both in selecting them and in strengthening
them. Here, again, we may take a leaf from St. Paul's
biography. Returning to Lystra and to Iconium and
Antioch, he, for the care of the souls, ordained them
elders in every church and prayed with fasting and
commended them to the Lord, on whom they believed
(Acts 14:21-23). Prayer is important for the selection
of spiritual leadership in the church, for prayer, if it
be earnest and sincere, opens the eyes and deepens
the understanding and leads to a ballot that is guided
in its choice by the standard set in the New Testament. Too often men are chosen to spiritual leadership in the church who do not lead exemplary Christian lives, who have no deep spirituality, no real
acquaintance with the Word of God or prayer, no
zeal for Christ, no passion for souls — but they are
well-to-do or popular or successful in their chosen
field, and so they are chosen. A tragedy! A foolish,
blundering tragedy, concerning which we can only
say, "But God meant it unto good, to bring to pass —"
(Genesis 50:20). The church needs spiritual leaders,
strong in faith, devoted to Christ, of Christian character, deeply taught in the Word of God, full of love
for their fellow believers, eager for the spread of the

123

Gospel and the salvation of souls. For such men as these we must pray. — And after they have been selected, they must be strengthened by our intercession for them that they may live lives commendable to their Master, that they may have abundant grace, humility, wisdom, vision, and energy and that all they do may bear the impress of Christ. Is it too high an ideal? Then pray — fervently — that it may be attained.

In our intercessions for the church at home we must never forget the pastor, for his labors are arduous and bear on them the imprint of eternity. St. Paul was always eager that his fellow Christians should pray for him, and from time to time he made requests that they should pray about definite matters concerning him and his work. He bade the saints at Rome "strive together with me in your prayers to God for me that I may be delivered from them that do not believe in Judea" (Romans 15:30, 31). He requests the believers at Colossae to continue steadfastly in prayer that God might open a door for the Word and that he, Paul, might set forth the Gospel clearly (Colossians 4:2-4). He invites the Thesslonians to pray that the Word of the Lord may have free course and be glorified (2 Thessalonians 3:1). He tells the Corinthians that they also are "helping together by prayer for us" (2 Corinthians 1:11). To be a successful soul winner the pastor needs the prayerful assistance and the assisting prayers of his parishioners.

We must not forget to pray for the church abroad. Come with me to a congregational meeting. I do not know the name of the church, except that this is the church where the believers in Jesus were first called Christians. The Holy Spirit has just selected Barnabas and Saul for the Gentile ministry; and the congregation has consented (Acts 13:1, 2). "And when they had fasted and prayed and laid their hands on them, they sent them away" (v. 3). And the two went forth, and as they prayed and preached, endured and labored, what a rich harvest of souls was theirs! Souls won for Christ in Cyprus, in Perga, in Pisidian Antioch, in Iconium, in Lystra, in Derbe. Souls as much prayed into the Kingdom as preached into it! In a very real sense the praying church in Syrian Antioch was the spiritual mother of these souls. It is a vision which, if we have caught it, will make us more fervent in our intercession for our missionaries and for the souls they seek to win for the Savior.

For whom should we pray? We have only begun the list. The very plethora of names which deserve to be listed compels us to combine them and to say: for the world, for the nations, for the government, for the President, for the Congress, for the commonwealth, for the governor, for the city, for the mayor, for the aldermen, for the men and women in service, for the schools, for the teachers, for the pupils, for the tempted, for the weak, for the sick, for the troubled, for all sorts and conditions of men. What a tremendous field! What a tremendous responsibility! If a sick person would have been restored through my intercessory prayer; if the afflicted would have been eased through my intercessory prayer; if a sinner would have been saved through my intercessory prayer, what a monstrous sin to have neglected it!

There come to mind the words of Samuel: "God forbid that I should sin against the Lord in ceasing to pray for you" (1 Samuel 12:23). But oh, again, the great honor done us by God to choose us to be workers together with Him, rulers together with Him through our intercessory prayers! God be praised! We have not deserved the honor. All the more should we appreciate it.

To help us remember the duty and the privilege of intercession we shall do well to make an intercession list, either mentally or on paper, of people and causes for which we want, and feel we ought, to pray. If the list is long, we may divide it and pray it according to the installment plan; and from time to time we will naturally want to revise the list.

This is a large field — intercessory prayer; but large as it is, there is no room here for men of small spirits. A self-centered man cannot pray for others. When we pray for others, the current of love must flow through us and through our prayers. This will make them effective; for love will know how to individualize the prayers, how to particularize them, how to personalize them, how to pinpoint them to their need.

THANKSGIVING AND PRAISE

Great is the mercy of our God — mercy that forgives us all our sins, mercy that helps us in time of need, mercy that supplies us with all our wants, mercy that gives us privileges which are not at all commensurate with our character! For this great mercy we owe Him thankfulness and praise. "Oh, give thanks unto the Lord, for He is good; because His mercy endureth forever." (Psalm 118:1)

Prayers of thanksgiving and praise could well have been considered in connection with prayers of adoration, for they are akin; and yet, because of their importance in the Christian's prayer life, they deserve a separate treatment; for whereas the prayer of adoration is the prayer "by which we express our sense of the goodness and greatness of God" and by which we pay homage to Him whom we hold in highest esteem, the prayer of thanksgiving and praise is the prayer "by which we express our gratitude to God" for all that He has done for us.

The complaint is often made that here is a prayer that is too often neglected. We grant the justice of the complaint, for gratitude is rare, indeed. Yet the charge, tacit in this complaint, needs to be examined lest we become guilty of generalizing.

Not every prayer of thanksgiving need contain an expression of thanks to be a prayer of thanksgiving. Except for the doxology even the Lord's Prayer does not contain such an expression; and even the doxology Jesus did not always add when He taught the prayer to His disciples (Luke 11:2-4). But the note of thanksgiving is not missing from the Lord's Prayer, not if we pray it as Luther advises us to pray it; for "God gives daily bread indeed without our prayer, also to all the wicked; but we pray in this petition that He would lead us to know it and to receive our daily bread with thanksgiving."

And yet we have reason to deplore "the coldness of our devotions." And we have so much for which

127

to be thankful! Big things? Yes, verily, big things! In summer the gentle coolness of the linen pillow slip as we lie down to rest. In winter the soothing warmth of the cover on our bed. In spring the sweet breath of mother earth fragrant with grasses and flowers and soft and generous as the mercy of God. In fall the flashing leaves of the trees fluttering in the breezes "like the tousled hair of children at play," trees which willingly yield us boards for our home and, in pity, a coffin for our grave. One of them one day bore a heavy burden. It lifted up the Son of God in pain to face the blazing sun, the frightening darkness, and the burning wrath of God. These are big things which we have come to take for granted but for which we ought daily to thank God, even as we thank Him for the rain and the sunshine, for our food and clothing, for our relatives and friends, for our strength, for our abilities, for our talents, for our successes, and for our opportunities to serve.

St. Paul sums it up nicely when he writes: "Giving thanks always for all things unto God and the Father in the name of our Lord Jesus Christ" (Ephesians 5:20). For all things? Shall I give thanks also for the bitter experiences of life? Shall I give thanks for sicknesses? Shall I give thanks for the loss of a dear one? Shall I give thanks for deep disappointments? Yes, indeed! Because I have in the name of Jesus Christ, who has redeemed me, become a child of the heavenly Father, I must give thanks unto God for all things. Am I sick — God is humbling me, drawing me away from the world, making me turn to Him. Is my loved one sick — God is drawing us closer together in His

128

name and nearer to heaven — together. Do I lose a loved one in death — God has given me an added attachment to heaven. Do I experience a bitter disappointment, keen and deep — God would teach me to do without that upon which I had set my heart and to learn anew that "God is the Strength of my heart and my Portion forever" (Psalm 73:26). I should give thanks to God for all things. For the Bible teaches us that literally all things work together for our good, whether we realize it at the time or not.

Closely akin to gratitude is praise, and our prayers of thanksgiving should be tinted with praise, even in days of distress. Among the "all things" St. Paul, no doubt, had in mind the ability to sing praises even in prison.

Come with me to Philippi. It is the midnight hour, but there is no darkness in the souls of Paul and Silas. "At midnight Paul and Silas prayed and sang praises unto God; and the prisoners heard them" (Acts 16:25). Listen to them as they raise their voices in loving devotion to Jesus Christ, rejoicing in the goodness of God, exulting in the healing of the slave girl, praying for Lydia and her friends, making intercession for the unsaved multitudes, making mention, methinks, of their fellow prisoners and of their jailer. Listen to them as they break into praise, singing with melody in their hearts unto the Lord, letting the walls re-echo to the joyous strains of redeemed and victorious saints. How like Paul, who was often down in a dungeon but never "down in the dumps"! Even in prison he could later write, "Rejoice in the Lord always; and again I say, Rejoice" (Philippians 4:4). These words of

St. Paul re-echo a strain taken from Psalm 33: "Rejoice in the Lord, O ye righteous; for praise is comely for the upright" (v. 1). Never should we, as Christians, misrepresent our Lord by sheer dolefulness. Praise befits us and our calling. Praise ought to be strongly and closely entwined in our hearts, our voices, and our lives; for "there is nothing like praise to express our thanksgiving, our trustfulness, and our rejoicing in the Lord."

In our prayer life we should do more praising, for according to all indications that is what we shall do in heaven. Let's practice.

MEDITATION

Our age is a whirligig. Feverishly we run around crying, "Hurry, hurry, work, work, act, act, do this, do that, don't think, don't pray, you haven't the time."

> *Said the Robin to the Sparrow,*
> *"I should really like to know*
> *Why these anxious human beings*
> *Rush about and worry so."*
>
> *Said the Sparrow to the Robin,*
> *"Friend, I think that it must be*
> *That they have no heavenly Father*
> *Such as cares for you and me."*

(Elizabeth Cheney, *Overheard in an Orchard*)

In such a day as ours it has become increasingly difficult to meditate; and yet meditation is an enriching, a refreshing experience, for by it our spiritual batteries are recharged at the powerhouse of heaven. Let us then, take time, and if necessary, let us take time out, to meditate and, as we meditate, to pray. "Let the words of my mouth and the meditation of my heart be acceptable in Thy sight, O Lord, my Strength and my Redeemer." (Psalm 19:14)

Though we in our day, because of prevailing conditions, seem to have little time to meditate, meditation is the form of prayer best suited to busy persons. The farmer can engage in meditation as he rides his tractor, the dairyman as he milks his cows, the housewife as she prepares her meals or vacuums the rugs, the pastor as he makes his sick calls or drives his car from house to house, the businessman and the laborer as they commute, and the child as he lazily sends the block of wood skipping down the dusty lane. It is a relaxing form of prayer.

Let's try it. Let us in prayerful meditation place ourselves in the boat with the Lord's disciples. We imagine for ourselves every detail of the scene. We hear the winds blowing through the sails and listen to the creaking of the ropes. The fury of the wind dashes the boat with waves, and we feel the constant spray of water against our straining faces. Already we are ankle-deep in water — and the water is rising! We bail the water, we pull on the oars! We sense the odor of the angry wind rushing down the gorge upon the open waters. We hear the roar of the storm. We watch the blinding flash of lightning. We see the boat filling with water up its entire length. We look; and there at the other end of the boat is Jesus, asleep on the cushion. We had just about forgotten about Him. Or has He forgotten about us? "Master" — we shake Him none too gently, for we are agitated — "do You not care if we go down with this boat?" It does our tattered nerves good to see Him calmly arise, rebuke the wind, and say to the sea, "Peace! Be still!" Those words quiet more than the storm on the Sea of Galilee. (Cp. Brown, p. 172)

> *Jesus, Savior, pilot me*
> *Over life's tempestuous sea;*
> *Unknown waves before me roll,*
> *Hiding rock and treacherous shoal.*
> *Chart and compass come from Thee:*
> *Jesus, Savior, pilot me.* (Edward Hopper)

There are so many subjects which lend themselves to meditation. David, a busy man no doubt, found it so, for he wrote of the man blessed of God, "His delight is in the law of the Lord; and in His law doth he meditate day and night" (Psalm 1:2). The Christ Child adored in the manger; Christ walking along the dusty road with His disciples; Christ talking with the Samaritan woman; Christ at the Last Supper; Christ praying in the garden; Christ on the cross; the risen, glorified Christ; the ascended Lord on His throne of glory; God who is Love; God who is Power; God who is Peace; the Bible passage suggested by the Scripture text calendar; or even the subject matter of last Sunday's sermon — these, and others, are all nourishing grist for the mill of meditation. The Sunday's sermon especially, into which the pastor has put much thought, deserves more reflective meditation than we usually give it. Recall what the pastor said, let God once more speak to you, determine how it applies to you, how it corrects or helps you, how it inspires you.

Never hurry your meditation. Do not be too eager to leave one thought for the other; linger in your meditation. Keep the thoughts and ponder them in your heart, one thought at a time. It is given you of God; take it and thank Him for it, and let Him tell you more about it. If the thought is a starting point that leads you into other thoughts, follow. God may be leading you. But as you follow and meditate, look, contemplate, resolve. You are praying. You are talking with God.

Even a child can meditate; and in its meditation it may be led by its mother to a Man with the kindest face a child has ever been privileged to see. There are other men around Him who try to push the mothers away. The child shrinks back as these important people say to its mother, "Why do you want to force your way? Can't you see that He is much too busy to be bothered with your children?" A voice, matching in gentle tone the kindness of its face, says, "Let the children come to Me, do not hinder them; for to such belongs the kingdom of God" (Mark 10:14 RSV). Encouraged, the timid child steps forward, and gently the Man lifts it up on His knee and speaks to it. The child snuggles close and prays,

> *Lord Jesus, who dost love me,*
> *Oh, spread Thy wings above me*
> *And shield me from alarm!*
> *Though evil would assail me,*
> *Thy mercy will not fail me:*
> *I rest in Thy protecting arm.*

(Paul Gerhardt)

Children do not meditate in that way? Don't they? I remember a boy, not yet in his teens, who meditated many a catechism lesson as he walked the cows up the lane from the pasture to the barn; and never was his heart more overwhelmed by the beauty of God's infinite grace as when, in answer to his meditation, there was revealed to him the truth, the lack of which so haunted Luther in his early years: "By grace are ye saved through faith, and that not of yourselves; it is the gift of God; not of works, lest any man should boast" (Ephesians 2:8, 9). The whelming has never left him!

He who knows how to meditate in prayer has experienced the glory of a walk with God, and by that experience he has heard an echo of the Paradise that was and has enjoyed a foretaste of the Paradise that will be.

EJACULATORY

If still you plead that you do not have time to pray, let me recommend to you what is spoken of as ejaculatory prayer. "Fragmentary prayers," someone has called them, "quick mental turnings to God." The *Lutheran Cyclopedia* describes them as "a short wish or an appeal addressed to God spontaneously springing from the mind." It is prayer that darts upward to God, not at stated times, but whenver our impulse moves us, or joy or sorrow strikes us, or a crisis calls for immediate action, or an interval gives time for thought. "Lord, I thank Thee for the beauty of the landscape!" "God be praised for all His goodness!"

"Lord, make me to understand the reason!" "Lord, help me!" "Lord, show me how!" "Oh, how good it is to be a child of God!" In his Large Catechism Luther under the Second Commandment speaks of "the practice of children to cross themselves when anything monstrous or terrible is seen or heard, and to exclaim: 'Lord God, protect us!' 'Help, dear Lord Jesus!' etc. Thus, too, if anyone meets with unexpected good fortune, however trivial, that he say: 'God be praised and thanked; this God has bestowed on me!' " Such brief prayers are valuable. This does not mean, of course, that we *should want to* dispense with longer prayers.

Nevertheless, such ejaculatory prayers will interlace without interference the often deadening details of the duties of the day with the thread of elevating and purifying and lightening thought; they will help to keep the soul steadfastly in harmony with the will of God; and they will save many an idle moment which otherwise would be wasted and sometimes worse than wasted. The busy person who makes ejaculatory prayer a habit need not at eventide meet his Savior as a stranger whom he has not met since the early hours of the morning.

If now you are still too busy to pray, then you are too busy. But you are not; and therefore you will pray:

> *O Thou by whom we come to God,*
> *The Life, the Truth, the Way,*
> *The path of prayer Thyself hast trod,*
> *Lord, teach us how to pray.* (Montgomery)

135

In the very nature of the case, if we follow St. Paul's precept to "pray without ceasing," most of our prayers will be private prayers. But God, who has made us social beings, does not want us to forget the social aspect of prayer.

IN THE HOME

The most important unit of society is the home. It needs to be bulwarked by prayer; for not only does the family which prays together stay together, it also stays closer to God.

The alarmists tell us that the practice of family worship (commonly called the family altar) is declining. But whether the family altar has been less popular in our days than in the eras before us, I have no way of judging. I believe that the family altar has never been as popular as it deserves to be. At the family altar the members of the household, parents and children and servants, speak to God not only individually but also as one united group whose relations to one another in the home are sacred. In particular, the head of the family, the pastor of the household (for he holds a pastorate there which he can never delegate to another), solemnly and openly declares himself a child of God, a believer in His Word, and a man who seeks to live a life of faith and righteousness, as he leads his family in worship and prayer.

Which is the best way of conducting family worship? I do not believe that we can speak of any one

136

way as being the best. Here I would say, "Each family to its own taste; and that may vary from time to time."

Luther has a wonderful suggestion "how the head of the family should teach his household to pray morning and evening." Writes he:

"In the morning when you get up, make the sign of the holy cross and say:

"In the name of the Father and of the Son and of the Holy Ghost. Amen.

"Then, kneeling or standing, repeat the Creed and the Lord's Prayer.

"If you choose, you may also say this little prayer:

"I thank Thee, my heavenly Father, through Jesus Christ, Thy dear Son, that Thou hast kept me this night from all harm and danger; and I pray Thee that Thou wouldst keep me this day also from sin and every evil, that all my doings and life may please Thee. For into Thy hands I commend myself, my body and soul, and all things. Let Thy holy angel be with me, that the wicked Foe may have no power over me. Amen.

"Then go joyfully to your work, singing a hymn, like that of the Ten Commandments, or whatever your devotion may suggest."

His evening prayer follows the same pattern.

Another family may want to follow the suggestions of the various books or pamphlets on family devotions which are frequently published. It stands to reason that in the selection of these devotional books or

137

booklets care should be exercised to purchase only those which are orthodox in purpose and content.

Another family may want to arrange its own form of worship, patterning it somewhat after the church services, including hymns, Bible reading with longer or shorter comment, and prayers in which they consider the frequent events of importance to the family.

Whether the family worship should be held in the morning, at noon, or in the evening depends on the circumstances and the predilection of the family.

IN THE CHURCH

Once a week, and at other stated times, we go to a building whose counterpart the psalmist and the prophets called "the house of God" (Psalm 42:4; Isaiah 2:3; Micah 4:2), and Isaiah and Jesus after him called "the house of prayer" (Isaiah 56:7; Matthew 21:13) — our beloved church. We go to worship and to pray.

Participation in public worship begins before we leave home. "Keep thy foot when thou goest to the house of God, and be more ready to hear" (Ecclesiastes 5:1). As for private prayer, so must we also prepare for group worship, perhaps even more so. The spirit of leisureliness, where at all possible, and especially the spirit of anticipation should dominate the early morning hours. The temptation to lie late in bed is an evil temptation on a Sunday morning, for it can lead only to hurry and confusion and to an evil habit of arriving at the portals of the house of

God all in a flurry wholly out of harmony with the
purpose of the vesper bells which pealed forth their
invitation the evening before (cp. Garrett, p. 117).
Take time, even if it takes some effort, to prepare your
spirit and to adorn yourself outwardly according to
the custom of the community, and go to church with
your family, ready to participate fully in the worship.
As you enter, if you have not done so before, pray,
"Send forth Thy Holy Spirit, O God, upon him who
speaks and upon all who worship here, that we may
praise Thee in our hearts and in our lives, to the
glory of Thy holy name. Amen." Join in the singing
of the hymns. Pray with the pastor and through him.
Listen to the sermon in the spirit of prayer, for God
is speaking to you through the preacher, according
to His promise, "He that heareth you heareth Me"
(Luke 10:16). As you kneel at the Lord's altar to
receive the bread and the wine, touched by the presence of Jesus, who is giving you His body to eat and
His blood to drink, remember how He died for you
and for others and rose again that you might have
life. And if then for the rest of the day you return
from time to time to the thoughts which were instilled
in you at the service, it will have been a day that
could not have been better spent. You will be among
those who say, "I was glad when they said unto me,
Let us go into the house of the Lord." (Psalm 122:1)

But why go to the house of prayer? Is not God
everywhere? Yes, indeed; therefore also in church.
Does not also the sun shine from horizon to horizon,
and yet the lens can concentrate the rays of the sun

for greater light and heat? It was when the disciples "were all with one accord in one place" that the Holy Spirit was given them in fulfillment of the promise given them by Jesus (Acts 2). Group worship, apart from being a part of the Christian's prayer life, has a most salutary effect on it. It is in the house of prayer that we learn not to pray alone. Our Lord taught us this same lesson when He gave us instructions on how to pray. All the appeals of the Lord's Prayer are put in the plural form. Jesus did not teach us to say, "My Father," but, "Our Father"; He did not teach us to say, "Give me my daily bread," but, "Give us our daily bread." Of this unification of prayer desires we have an actual demonstration in group prayer. Ours is even the privilege of participating in it.

Group prayer, then, is a great factor in cementing the bond of union between pastor and people, between believer and fellow believers, and all with the souls that have gone before — the church of the ages. The people become more precious to their pastor as he prays for them, and the pastor becomes dearer to his people as they hear him pouring out his intercessions for them and for others. Each becomes more concerned for the highest welfare of the other. Prayer binds them together in a beautiful covenant of faith and affection, each to each, and all to God.

> *Before our Father's throne*
> *We pour our ardent prayers,*
> *Our fears, our hopes, our aims, are one,*
> *Our comfort and our cares.* (John Fawcett)

140

The prayer which each of us prays ascends, not as the lonely, solitary voice of one selfish individual but as a tiny part of that vast cloud of incense which rises from the heart of the universal church of God. And if God appreciates the individual prayer solo, certainly He will appreciate the symphony of public prayer.

Schedule of Prayer

Now as to a schedule of prayer, there is little to say. It is impossible to lay down rules, since none have been laid down by God. Yet it is a wise procedure for a Christian to adopt some schedule of prayer, to set what some call "fixed times" for prayer, and to exercise what others call "discipline," however not so as to restrict his prayer life to that schedule; for even if he has adopted a schedule, he will want to intersperse that schedule with other and perhaps frequent moments of prayer.

Many people — whether it be the majority, I do not care to say — have no fixed times for prayer. They have a fixed time for arising, a fixed time for their meals, a fixed time for their business, a fixed time for their games, a fixed time for their meetings, a fixed time to retire, but for prayer they do not have a fixed time. They regard prayer as a thing of the mood and to be practiced only when they feel in the mood for it. All is well, if their mood is not too moody.

A prayer schedule, certain fixed times of the day when we are accustomed to pray, is an important aid to the Christian's prayer life. It is especially important for those whose life is so full that prayer is in danger of being ruled out. They must definitely schedule their life so as to rule prayer back in. But this must not be overdone. The schedule must not become so rigid that its rigidity becomes a matter of conscience, lest prayer become a "yoke of bondage" to fear. If a person prays only by the aid of his watch, chances are that he will pray not much better than the watch — perfunctorily. Yet it has always been considered the Christian thing to do, to observe certain regular times for prayer.

The saints of old observed such regular times for prayer. The psalmist mentions "seven times a day" (Psalm 119:164), and on this the medieval church based the seven canonical hours of prayer. It is quite likely, though, that the number seven is here used as a round number simply meaning "several." More precise, no doubt, is David in another Psalm: "Evening and morning and at noon will I pray" (Psalm 55:17). This trilogy reminds us of Daniel's custom of praying "three times a day" (Daniel 6:10). But whatever the number may be, each one should for himself insist on definite and regular times of prayer and, if possible, let nothing interfere with them.

Morning, noon, and night is a good schedule. In the morning, as we look forward to the duties of the day, anticipate the many situations in which temptations may lurk, and prepare to embrace such opportunities as may offer themselves for service, nothing is better than to take God into our confidence.

142

With the Lord begin thy task,
Jesus will direct it;
For His aid and counsel ask,
Jesus will perfect it.
Every morn with Jesus rise,
And when day is ended,
In His name then close thine eyes;
Be to Him commended.

Let each day begin with prayer,
Praise and adoration;
On the Lord cast every care,
He is thy Salvation.
Morning, evening, and at night
Jesus will be near thee,
Save thee from the Tempter's might,
With His presence cheer thee.

The noontide, which breaks up the busy day, may be more than just a coffee break. The least we can do is to remember the word of St. Paul: "Whether therefore ye eat or drink, or whatsoever ye do, do all to the glory of God" (1 Corinthians 10:31). He would not have us take the bounty of God for granted. He would commend to us the practice of grace before meals, a custom at present more honored in the breach than in the observance. We began the day with Him, why not continue with Him, and pray:

Come, Lord Jesus, be our Guest,
And let these gifts to us be blest.

The evening hour — this is the time to relax. The heat and the burden of the day are past. The troubled skeins are untangled, the hurt and the fret are taken out of the heart, the burdens and anxieties are rolled on God, who has invited us to cast our care upon

143

Him, for He careth for us (1 Peter 5:7). The day is far spent, and the time for rest draws near. We have walked with God today, and now we invite our gracious Companion,

Abide with me! Fast falls the eventide;
The darkness deepens; Lord, with me abide.
When other helpers fail and comforts flee,
Help of the helpless, oh, abide with me. . . .

Hold Thou Thy cross before my closing eyes,
Shine through the gloom, and point me to
   the skies.
Heaven's morning breaks, and earth's vain
   shadows flee;
In life, in death, O Lord, abide with me!"

(Henry Lyte)

With Him we enter the chamber of rest, and, as the curtains of night are drawn, we softly fall asleep, while the Lord's holy angel is with us, that the wicked Foe may have no power over us. Amen.

ACKNOWLEDGMENTS

The author herewith gratefully acknowledges his indebtedness to the following publishers for their generous permission to quote material from copyrighted books. In some instances words and phrases were borrowed and incorporated into the author's material without specifically indicating their original source.

Growth in Prayer, by Constance Garrett. Copyright 1949, 1950, by the Macmillan Co., New York. Fifth printing, 1956.

In the Secret Place of the Most High, by Arthur J. Gossip. Copyright 1947 by Charles Scribner's Sons, New York.

The Way of Prayer, by Charles Ewing Brown. Copyright 1940 by the author. Third printing published 1950 by Warner Press, Anderson, Ind.

"Overheard in an Orchard," by Elizabeth Cheney. Copyright 1920 by the *Sunday School Times.*